THE CREATIVE POWER
OF PRAYER

THE CREATIVE POWER OF PRAYER

EDITED AND PUBLISHED BY SHEKINAH EDITIONS

WRITTEN BY PASTOR
MARIANA VANSTIPELEN

THE CREATIVE POWER OF PRAYER

Scriptures mainly quoted from King James and
New King James Versions of Th e Bible.

© 2025 By Shekinah Editions

Cover and Content Design: Marcin & Milou
Production and Printing: Drukcase
Author: Mariana Vanstipelen
Publisher: Shekinah Editions
Paperback ISBN: 979-8-899-89057-4

DEDICATION

When God wants to bless you,
when He longs to draw you closer,
to glorify Himself in and through you,
He stirs within you a desire to pray.

This book has found its way into your hands for a reason:
to ignite a new passion in your prayer life,
to open doors to your divine destiny and
to empower you to overcome any obstacles to prayer.

May this book inspire you to draw nearer to God,
find victory over prayerlessness, and
walk boldly in the purposes God has prepared for you.

To the boundless grace and infinite goodness of the Lord,
we dedicate this book.

GLORY TO GOD!!

PREFACE

Thanks be to God Almighty for His tender mercies and loving-kindness that have sustained us through the many challenges faced in planting churches in cities where opposition to the work of God was evident.

Yet, to the glory of God, they could not resist His will.

The Lord Jesus speaking to the apostle Paul at his conversion in *Acts 9:5 "And he said, Who art thou, Lord? And the Lord said, I am Jesus whom thou persecutest: it is hard for thee to kick against the pricks. (KJV)*

The Church overcomes through prayers.

Matthew 16:18 *"And I say also unto thee, That thou art Peter, and upon this rock I will build my church; and the gates of hell shall not prevail against it."*

When I was a young believer, I often pondered the meaning of the "gates of hell." I wondered, "Are there literal gates in hell, and how do they relate to the Church?"

One day, through His mercy, the Lord gave me clarity. The gates of hell represent the agents of satan, whether in human or demonic form. These forces often operate within the Church or close to God's children outside, with the sole purpose of drawing Christians away from the Church and back into the world, ultimately leading them to eternal separation from God. These agents act as gateways to hell itself, hence the term "gates of hell."

But take heart, for the Lord Jesus Christ assured us that they will not prevail against His Church.

"And I say also unto thee, That thou art Peter, and upon this rock I will build my church; and the gates of hell shall not prevail against it." Matthew 16:18 Hallelujah!

We pray that believers embrace the vital tool God has given us called PRAYER.

Living a life grounded in prayer is the key to a victorious life filled with peace, righteousness, and joy in the Holy Spirit. Prayer empowers you to overcome spiritual battles and compels you to glorify the Name of God.

In this book, we are speaking about the creative power of prayer.

Toward the end of this book, you'll find an overview of Pastor Mariana's collection of works. Each title is to deepen your understanding and enhance your spiritual journey. We invite you to explore these resources, which are available by theme and title. Copies can be requested through our website, where you'll find further details to continue growing in faith and knowledge.

www.shekinahevangelicalchurch.com

GOD BLESS YOU AS YOU KEEP PRAYING.

TABLE OF CONTENTS

*"Call unto Me, and I will answer thee,
and show thee great and mighty things,
which thou knowest not."*

JEREMIAH 33: 3

PRAYER IS THE KEY TO VICTORY.

INTRODUCTION

THE PRINCIPLES OF OUR LORD JESUS CHRIST

A principle is a law or rule that must be followed, whether willingly or out of necessity, for the well-being of all.

The principles of our Lord Jesus Christ are distinct from His sacrificial works. The sacrificial works that Jesus Christ undertook were to serve as a ransom for our sins.

As Matthew 1: 21 says, *"She will bring forth a Son, and you shall call His name JESUS, for He will save His people from their sins."*

Our Lord does not require us to repeat His sacrificial works today, for He is the Lamb who was slain once and for all.

The Lord Jesus Christ, in His divine mission, came down from Heaven and was born of a virgin, a miraculous birth, pure and untouched by any man. This extraordinary event marked the beginning of His earthly ministry. But is He asking us to replicate this by being born through virgins in mangers today? No. His birth was a unique fulfilment of prophecy, an event that underscored His divine nature and purpose.

Jesus Christ willingly endured immense suffering at Calvary. He was nailed to a wooden cross, bearing the weight of humanity's sins. This act of ultimate sacrifice was the means by which He provided salvation for all. Are we, as His followers, required to undergo physical crucifixion on a wooden cross today? No. His sacrifice was once for all, a singular event that cannot and need not be repeated. Christ reclaimed the dominion which Adam had lost in the Garden of Eden. This victory was a turning point in the spiritual realm, securing our freedom from the bondage of sin.

Jesus accomplished this victory on our behalf, and now we stand in the authority of His triumph, fighting our spiritual battles through faith, prayer, and the power of His Name. Obviously, we are not expected to perform these same sacrificial acts today because the Lord Jesus fulfilled them once and for all.

After His resurrection, the Lord Jesus Christ ascended to Heaven, witnessed by His disciples, and took His place at the Throne of the Father, where He now sits at His right hand, interceding for us. Hallelujah!

All these works are a free gift; a divine act of grace, a sacrifice offered on our behalf to pay the ransom for our sins, a debt we could never repay for our own redemption.

Yet, as Christians, there are fundamental but crucial principles that we are expected to follow. The Lord Himself calls us to adhere to them for our own good.

Indeed, the entire counsel of God concerning Christianity is built upon these principles, which we refer to as the Principles of the Lord Jesus.

It is my responsibility, as well as that of all Christians, to emphasize these principles so that they can be effectively implemented in the lives of God's children and in the Church of God around the world today.

These three foundational principles are: Prayer, Fasting, and Charity.

In this book, we focus on: The principle of prayer, specifically exploring

THE CREATIVE POWER OF PRAYER.

Prayer is a profound mystery and a remarkable gift; a sacred invitation to commune with God: The Creator of all. Through prayer, we enter into God's presence, engage in dialogue with Him, and are transformed by His love, wisdom, and power. Yet, prayer is more than a spiritual practice; it is a life-giving connection that shapes who we are, aligns us with God's purpose, and brings heaven's influence into our lives on earth.

In *The Creative Power of Prayer*, we journey beyond a surface-level understanding of prayer to explore its dynamic, its creative force that can shape our destiny, impact our society, and bring the Kingdom of God closer to those around us.

In a world filled with constant demands, and challenges, prayer becomes a sanctuary; a place to, recharge, and realign with God's heart. It is here, in moments of honest prayer, that we experience the peace and strength that come from being in His presence. Through prayer, we have the privilege of bringing our struggles, fears, hopes, and dreams before the One who knows us intimately and has plans of great purpose for our lives. As we pray, we are not only heard by God but actively strengthened, renewed, and empowered to walk in His ways.

This book explores prayer as both a divine privilege and a call to action. In the Bible, we see that prayer is an essential part of the lives of those who walked closely with God. Jesus, our ultimate example, modelled a life of prayer, often withdrawing from crowds to connect deeply with His Father. The apostles, too, embraced the transformative power of prayer, gathering daily to seek God's will, support one another, and find strength to advance the gospel, even in the face of persecution. Through their commitment, the early Church experienced miracles, signs, and wonders that flowed from a life saturated in prayer. Their example teaches us that prayer is a powerful tool God has given us to shape our world, overcome the enemy, and fulfil the callings He has placed on our lives.

The creative power of prayer lies in its ability to bring about God's purposes in our lives and the lives of others. When we pray, we release God's plans for healing, provision, and transformation over our families, workplaces, communities, and nations. Prayer allows us to participate in God's work, transforming our hearts and positioning us as His vessels, through whom His love and power can flow. It is through prayer that we can engage in God's mission and bring hope, light, and change to a world in need.

But prayer is also a journey of growth and intimacy. As we move beyond the initial steps of asking and seeking, we discover deeper levels of communion, where God's voice becomes clear, His guidance more precise, and His will more discernible. We begin to see prayer not only as a means to receive answers but as a place to surrender, allowing God to shape our character, increase our faith, and cultivate our dependence on Him. Here, we encounter the Holy

Spirit's power, the creativity of God's guidance, and the empowerment to live with purpose.

Through this book, I pray that you will be stirred to embrace prayer with renewed passion and commitment. You will learn how to cultivate a prayer life that is both disciplined and spontaneous, founded on God's Word, led by the Holy Spirit, and anchored in faith. We will explore the beauty of a life transformed by prayer and the countless promises God has for us when we align with His word.

Let this book serve as your invitation to enter into a life of powerful, transformative prayer; a life where you can hear from God, witness His miracles, and experience the full depth of His love and purpose for you. As you walk through each chapter, may you find yourself growing in strength, wisdom, and joy, and may your journey in prayer bring you ever closer to the heart of the Father. May this be the season where your prayers become a creative force, shaping not only your own life but the lives of all those you touch.

The Lord stands ready to meet you, guide you, and empower you. As you enter this journey, may you discover that prayer is not only a way to communicate with God but a place of profound transformation, empowerment, and joy. A place where His will becomes your will, His desires your desires, and His power flows through you to accomplish great things. May *The Creative Power of Prayer* be a tool that strengthens, inspires, and equips you to pray like never before. Let us begin this journey of creative, powerful, and life-changing prayer together.

CHAPTER 1

THE EARLY CHURCH AND PRAYER

CHAPTER 1

THE EARLY CHURCH AND PRAYER

PRAYER IN THE EARLY CHURCH: A FOUNDATION OF POWER

In the book of Acts, we witness the birth of the early church on the day of Pentecost, a pivotal moment in the history of Christianity. The believers were united in prayer, fervently seeking the promise of the Holy Spirit as instructed by the Lord Jesus. This was not just an ordinary gathering but a demonstration of faith in action. Jesus had promised them that the Holy Spirit would come to empower them for the mission ahead, and they did not waver in their expectation. It was in this atmosphere of prayer that the Holy Spirit descended upon them, marking the beginning of the Church's mission to spread the gospel.

This moment reveals the truth about the power of prayer in birthing God's purposes on earth. The believers, gathered in one accord, prayed with expectancy, and through their prayer, the Holy Spirit was released to empower them for the work ahead. This is a profound example of how prayer plays a creative role in establishing God's kingdom. Without prayer, the Church would not have experienced the outpouring of the Holy Spirit in such a transformative way.

I often emphasize the significance of the numbers involved on that day. The Lord Jesus had twelve disciples, and on the day of Pentecost, they were multiplied. This serves as a powerful illustration of what the Church could look like today if each believer took responsibility for discipling others. If each Christian were to win at least ten souls to Christ, the Church would multiply exponentially. This multiplication, however, is not just about numerical growth but about the spiritual transformation that comes when believers are empowered through prayer and the Holy Spirit.

To see this kind of growth, we need to take a page from the early Church's book. The early believers were persistent, fervent, and effective in prayer. They didn't rely on human strength or strategies; they depended on the power of the Holy Spirit, which was accessed through prayer. The results were evident: they spread the Word of God with signs and wonders following, and the Church grew daily. This brings to light the importance of persistent prayer in bringing about spiritual growth and expansion.

Prayer was not a secondary activity for the early Church; it was their lifeline. It was the means through which they connected with God's power, received His guidance, and experienced His miraculous intervention. The early Church teaches us that effective prayer is the foundation for any lasting impact. If we, the modern Church, are to see similar results, we must become a praying Church once again. We must prioritize prayer as the engine that drives our mission and the source of power that enables us to witness the transformation of lives.

In today's context, this call to persistent, fervent prayer is more relevant than ever. As believers, we are tasked with reaching a world that is increasingly distant from God. Like the early Church, we cannot accomplish this mission in our own strength. We need the creative power of prayer to unlock heaven's resources, empower us with the Holy Spirit, and equip us to reach the lost with boldness and effectiveness.

The early Church's example challenges us to reevaluate our priorities. Are we relying on our own abilities, or are we seeking the Lord in prayer, trusting in His power to move? As we pray, we partner with God in bringing His Kingdom to earth, just as the early believers did on the day of Pentecost. This is the creative power of prayer, through it, we bring forth God's will and purposes in the world. Just as the early Church grew through the power of prayer and the Holy Spirit, we too can see tremendous growth and transformation when we make prayer our priority.

In Acts 4: 24, 29 – 31, we read regarding the power of prayer:

"And when they heard that, they lifted up their voice to God with one accord, and said, Lord, Thou art God, which hast made heaven, and earth, and the sea, and all that in them is: … And now, Lord, behold their threatenings: and grant unto thy servants, that with all boldness they may speak Thy Word, By stretching forth Thine Hand to heal; and that signs and wonders may be done by the Name of Thy Holy Child Jesus. And when they had prayed, the place was shaken where they were assembled together; and they were all filled with the Holy Ghost, and they spake the Word of God with boldness."

We need to pray with the same fervency and effectiveness today to have a significant impact on the world around us and win as many souls as possible back to The Lord.

The calling we have as believers is a monumental one. We have been commissioned to be active participants in God's redemptive plan on earth. At the heart of this mission is a relentless battle against the enemy of our souls; the devil. The Bible makes it clear that there is an adversary who actively works to deceive and keep people in bondage. Yet, we are called to overcome him, not through our human strength, but through the power of God working in and through us.

The mandate is clear: we are to bring as many souls as possible into the knowledge of God, rescuing them from the snares of the enemy. Every soul that is won for Christ is a victory against the forces of darkness. The devil's ultimate goal is to keep as many people as possible away from God. But our role as believers is to reverse this, to plunder the darkness world, depopulate it, and populate God's Kingdom. Our prayers are integral to this process. In prayer, we engage with the divine power that has already conquered sin, death, and satan. We draw on that victory, applying it to the lives of those we pray for, and opening the way for God's will to be done on earth as it is in Heaven.

This task of intercession and spiritual warfare is not something we undertake lightly. It is a privilege. The fact that we can approach the throne of God and partner with Him in bringing about His purposes on the earth is nothing short of awe-inspiring. Prayer allows us to work alongside the Creator of the universe in the unfolding of His plan. This awareness should humble us deeply. It should remind us that we are utterly dependent on Him. The battle we fight is spiritual, and as such, it cannot be won with earthly weapons or strategies. It requires the intervention of God Himself. Through prayer, we express our dependence on Him, acknowledging that without His strength, His wisdom, and His intervention, we can do nothing.

Prayer, then, is both a privilege and a necessity. It is a privilege because God, in His grace, invites us into His presence. It is a necessity because without it, we are powerless against the enemy. The enemy is relentless, but so must we be in our prayers. Scripture exhorts us to "pray without ceasing" (1 Thessalonians 5:17). This is not just a suggestion; it is an imperative. The nature of spiritual warfare requires constant vigilance. The enemy is always at work, seeking to steal, kill, and destroy (John 10:10). Therefore, we must be just as persistent, ensuring that our prayers are continuous, fervent, and effective.

In practice, praying without ceasing means cultivating a lifestyle of prayer. It means that prayer is not confined to a particular time of day or a specific location. Rather, it becomes a natural part of our everyday lives, flowing in and out of everything we do. Yet, while we strive to maintain this attitude of constant prayer, the reality is that the busyness of life often intrudes. Our schedules fill up quickly, and before we know it, the day has passed without us having spent any significant time in prayer.

It is at this point that we must take intentional steps to reorder our priorities. If our current schedule leaves little to no space for prayer, then something needs to change. We need to recognize that prayer is not optional for the believer; it is essential. There is nothing wrong with adjusting our schedules to make room for prayer. In fact, it is a sign of wisdom and maturity. Just as we would adjust our schedules for other important tasks or meetings, so too should we rearrange our time to ensure that we are making space for communion with God.

Rescheduling to prioritize prayer may mean different things for different people. For some, it might involve waking up earlier in the morning to spend time with God before the demands of the day begin. For others, it could mean setting aside specific times during the day for short, focused moments of prayer. Still, others may need to designate a quiet space in the evening where they can meet with God in uninterrupted prayer. Whatever the solution may be, the key is to be intentional about creating space for prayer. This is not about legalism or rigid routines, but about recognizing the absolute necessity of being in constant communion with God.

Moreover, this rescheduling is not just for the sake of personal spiritual growth. It is for the sake of the Kingdom. Every time we pray, we are participating in the advancement of God's Kingdom on earth. Our prayers are not limited by time or space; they reach into the heavens and have a direct impact on the spiritual realm. When we pray for the salvation of souls, we are aligning ourselves with God's heart and His ultimate desire; that none should perish, but that all should come to repentance (2 Peter 3: 9).

Prayer becomes, therefore, a powerful tool in the hands of every believer. Through prayer, we push back the forces of darkness and create space for God's light to shine in the lives of those around us. We stand in the gap for those who are still lost, interceding on their behalf and asking God to open their eyes to the truth. The more we engage in this kind of prayer, the more we weaken the enemy's hold on the people of this world.

In a very real sense, we are called to make hell desolate. The enemy's plans are to fill hell with as many souls as possible, but through prayer and the preaching of the gospel, we disrupt those plans. Every time a soul is saved, hell loses a captive, and Heaven gains a citizen. This is the ultimate goal of our spiritual warfare not just to overcome the enemy in our personal lives, but to see his kingdom dismantled and God's Kingdom established in the lives of others.

And all of this is made possible through the creative power of prayer. Prayer not only changes circumstances, it changes people. It breaks the chains of bondage, heals the broken hearted, and opens the eyes of the blind. It is through prayer that we partner with God in bringing about His purposes on the earth, in rescuing souls from the grip of the enemy, and in filling heaven with those who have been redeemed by the blood of the Lamb.

In the early Church, believers were deeply committed to prayer, structuring their day around specific times of devotion, such as 09 am, 12 midday, and 3 pm. This rhythm of prayer mirrors the practice of the prophet Daniel, who prayed at least three to five times daily despite his demanding role as a high-ranking servant of the king. His discipline in prayer, regardless of his responsibilities, gives a key lesson for believers: prayer should be a non-negotiable priority in our daily lives. Daniel's dedication to prayer offers a practical and spiritual framework. His consistency teaches us the importance of setting aside time for prayer, free from distractions, and being resolute in communicating with God. Even in the busyness of life, when responsibilities seem overwhelming, Daniel's example shows that it is possible to maintain a fervent prayer life if we value communion with God above all else. His devotion speaks of an understanding that no earthly duty is more critical than time spent in God's presence.

Many people today might feel unsure about how to pray, but just as we learn other skills, prayer is something we can develop by studying the Bible and paying attention to how God speaks to us through His Word. The scriptures provide a wealth of guidance, revealing God's desires and His will for our lives. As we read the Word, we begin to understand how to align our prayers with His purposes.

Furthermore, the Holy Spirit is the key Helper in this process. Romans 8: 26 assures us that the Spirit helps us in our weaknesses, especially when we do not know what to pray. By seeking the Spirit's guidance, we are empowered to pray according to God's will, allowing our prayers to be more effective and meaningful. This divine partnership enables us to not only pray with boldness but also with precision, knowing that our prayers are in line with what God desires.

Additionally, we can look to the apostles and their prayer lives in the early Church. Acts 2: 42 shows us that the apostles devoted themselves to prayer and to the teaching of the Word. Their prayers were marked by persistence, faith, and a deep reliance on the power of the Holy Spirit. By emulating their practices, we can develop a richer and more disciplined prayer life.

Incorporating regular prayer into our lives, just as Daniel and the early believers did, invites a deeper intimacy with God. Prayer, when scheduled and made a priority, becomes not just an act of devotion but a creative force that shapes our spiritual growth and fuels the advancement of God's Kingdom. As we commit to this practice, we cultivate a lifestyle that places God at the centre of everything we do, reinforcing an unbreakable connection with God.

THE THREE LEVELS OF PRAYER

In Matthew 7:7, Jesus offers profound instruction on prayer: *"Ask, and it shall be given you; seek, and ye shall find; knock, and it shall be opened unto you."* This simple yet powerful verse outlines three progressive levels of engagement with God, each representing a deepening relationship with Him through prayer.

The Asking Level

The asking level is the foundational stage of prayer, where we bring our requests to God. It is akin to communicating with Him from the comfort of our personal space, like talking to a friend. This is where many people begin their prayer journey, asking for their needs, desires, and help in times of trouble. It is an intimate and personal conversation with God, where the believer simply presents their requests.

At this level, our posture is less about the physical state and more about the heart's condition. You can be in any position whether lying in bed, sitting on a couch, or walking. It's a moment of honest communication with God, acknowledging His ability to provide and His willingness to respond. Asking may seem elementary, but it's crucial in establishing a relationship where you trust that God is listening and will act in accordance with His will.

Jesus encourages us to ask because it is a recognition of our dependence on Him. When we ask, we acknowledge that all we need comes from Him. This level of prayer builds faith as we see God answering our petitions, reinforcing our understanding that He hears and responds.

The Seeking Level

The seeking level is a deeper pursuit of God, where prayer becomes more than just asking for things; it becomes a quest to know Him. Here, believers move beyond their personal space and take active steps to encounter God in a more profound way, often by seeking Him in the house of God, in communal prayer, or through studying His Word.

Many believers find themselves here, seeking not just solutions to problems but the very presence of God Himself. In this stage, the focus shifts from personal needs to a deeper relationship with God. It is not enough to receive; we now want to understand and experience the fullness of who God is. As the psalmist says, *"When You said, 'Seek My face,' my heart said to You, 'Your face, Lord, I will seek.'"* (Psalm 27: 8).

The seeking stage is transformative because the more you seek God, the more He reveals Himself to you. It is a journey of discovery, where persistent prayer leads to a greater understanding of God's character, His will, and His purpose for your life. This pursuit might require sacrifice of time, energy, and focus, but it promises great reward: the joy of knowing God intimately.

The Knocking Level

The knocking level represents the most intense and persistent form of prayer. It involves a kind of spiritual warfare, where the believer engages in fervent, unyielding prayer until something changes. This is where Jesus operated and still operates consistently, and it is an example we are called to follow.

Knocking signifies perseverance. Just as Jacob wrestled with God and said, *"I will not let You go unless You bless me"* (Genesis 32: 26), so too must we persist in prayer until we receive breakthrough. Jesus exemplified this in His prayer life. In John 17, we see His intercession for His disciples and all believers; a prayer of deep significance. This kind of prayer is not casual; it is a determined pursuit of God's intervention.

In the knocking stage, the believer refuses to give up, continually "knocking" on Heaven's door. It is a place of deep intercession where you give God no rest until something happens (Isaiah 62: 7). This is the realm of spiritual breakthroughs, where you contend in prayer until the answer comes.

Each of these levels: asking, seeking, and knocking represents a progression in the believer's prayer life. As you grow in prayer, you move from simple requests to an intense desire for God's presence, and finally, to unrelenting intercession that brings

Heaven's realities to earth. These stages are not meant to be isolated but intertwined, showing the dynamic power of prayer that Jesus encourages us to embrace. The asking level teaches dependence, the seeking level shows intimacy, and the knocking level demonstrates perseverance. Together, they form a complete picture of a powerful and effective prayer life.

The Prayer that Brings Revival

In the book of Acts, we find the account of the disciples gathered in the upper room, waiting for the promised Holy Spirit (Acts 1: 13-15). Jesus had instructed them to remain in Jerusalem until they were *"endued with power from on high"* (Luke 24: 49). Their waiting was not passive; it was an intense and unified period of prayer. They poured out their hearts before God, knowing that without the Power of the Holy Spirit, they could not fulfil the great commission Jesus had entrusted to them.

This type of prayer is fervent, expectant, and persistent; a model for the Church in every generation.

The disciples didn't simply pray casually or with routine words. They prayed from the depths of their hearts, expressing their need for divine intervention. For days, they stayed together in prayer, seeking God's face with one mind and purpose, not giving up until they received what Jesus had promised.

This kind of focused, communal, and continuous prayer ultimately brought revival. It wasn't only the length of time that mattered but the intensity, sincerity, and unity of their prayers.

It is essential to recognize that the disciples didn't rush away from the upper room to take care of other matters; they didn't allow the distractions of everyday life to pull them away from the urgency of their spiritual need. They remained in God's presence, in one place and one accord, until the Holy Spirit came upon them like flames of fire. This is a lesson for the modern Church: Revival comes when God's people are willing to set aside distractions and commit themselves fully to seeking Him in prayer.

CHARACTERISTICS OF REVIVAL-PRAYER

1. Unified and Continuous Prayer

The first essential element of the disciples' prayer in the upper room was its unified nature. They all prayed together in one accord (Acts 1:14). The power of corporate prayer cannot be overstated. When believers come together, sharing the same vision, goal, and heart's cry, their prayers are amplified in the spiritual atmosphere. There is strength in numbers, especially when it comes to prayer.

The fact that they did not leave or give up also demonstrates the importance of persistence. Sometimes, breakthrough comes only when we are willing to pray without ceasing (1 Thessalonians 5:17), refusing to quit until we see God's promise fulfilled.

This is the kind of prayer that brings revival: a prayer that doesn't relent, that seeks God with a heart full of faith, knowing He is faithful to answer.

2. Heartfelt Prayer

Another key characteristic of the prayer in the upper room was its sincerity. The disciples didn't just recite pre-written prayers or offer up empty words. They prayed from their hearts. Heartfelt prayer is the kind of prayer that reaches God's throne. It is authentic, born from a deep hunger for God and an understanding of one's absolute dependence on Him.

The disciples had been with Jesus; they knew what it was like to experience His power and authority, and now they were seeking more of that power to fulfil His mission. This is the kind of prayer that brings revival in a church, city, or country: when people pray with all their heart, not for selfish motives but for the Kingdom of God to advance, for souls to be saved, and for God's glory to be revealed.

3. Spirit-Led and Expectant

The disciples were not praying out of ritual. They were waiting expectantly for what Jesus had promised them; The Holy Spirit. They didn't know exactly what that would look like, but they prayed with faith, trusting that God would send His Spirit in His perfect timing. This expectant prayer is crucial in ushering revival. It is the kind of prayer that doesn't just ask but seeks and knocks, pressing into God's will and purposes until heaven responds (Matthew 7:7).

True revival prayer is always Spirit-led. It goes beyond human understanding or desires and taps into the very heart of God. The disciples, after all, were in the upper room by the direction of Jesus Himself. They had received a Word from Him, and they obeyed it. Their prayer was aligned with God's will, and that is why it bore such tremendous fruit.

The Power of Persistent, Unified Prayer

When the Holy Spirit finally descended upon the disciples on the day of Pentecost, it was like tongues of fire resting on each of them (Acts 2: 3-4). That moment marked the birth of the Church, and it came as a direct result of persistent, unified, heartfelt prayer. The Holy Spirit's power enabled them to preach boldly, and thousands were added to the Church that day.

The same kind of revival that was experienced on the day of Pentecost can be experienced today in churches, cities, and nations if believers are willing to engage in the same kind of prayer. Revival is born in the place of persistent prayer, and it is sustained by a community of believers united in purpose and passionate about seeing God's kingdom come.

When we dedicate ourselves to prayer, refusing to give up until we see God move, we set the stage for revival. The power that fell on the disciples in the upper room is still available to the Church today.

If we pray like they prayed with one heart, one mind, and a burning desire for the Holy Spirit's outpouring, God will move once again with His transforming power.

The Deeper Level of Intimacy in Prayer

As we progress in our prayer life, there is a depth where we transition from simply asking and seeking God's face to being fully immersed in His presence. This stage is not about words anymore; it is about experiencing God in a powerful, transformative way. This is where prayer becomes more than a routine; it becomes an encounter with the living God.

Entering the Place of Spiritual Revelation

In this deeper connection with God, you are no longer confined to earthly limitations. Instead, God draws you into His presence in the Spirit. At this level, you begin to see visions, hear the voice of God clearly, and understand His divine purposes in ways that surpass human understanding. Your thoughts, time, and life are invested entirely in the Kingdom of God because your relationship with Him has moved from casual to intimate. Prayer at this level changes your life because you begin to operate with a higher understanding of spiritual things. No longer are the practices of the faith just something you follow out of obligation. Instead, it becomes a privilege and an honour to serve and worship God. Your entire being starts to revolve around God's will. You dance, you speak, and you constantly knock on Heaven's door, not out of need, but out of love and devotion to Him. The transformation is evident: it is no longer about what God can do for you, but about who He is and what He desires to accomplish through you.

Becoming a Vessel in God's Hands

As you surrender more deeply to God in prayer, you become His instrument, fully yielded to His will. At this stage, it is no longer about you, but about Christ living in you. Your prayer life reflects this shift. You no longer pray like someone in the early stages of asking or seeking, but as someone who has knocked on God's door and has been invited in. Your prayers change from "Lord, I seek You, show me Your face" to confident declarations, knowing that you have entered into God's presence and have His attention. Hallelujah!

This is the place where God desires us to be; a place of power, intimacy, and divine revelation. When you leave that sacred time of prayer, just like Moses coming down from Mount Sinai, the Shekinah Glory of God will shine on your forehead. The spiritual authority you carry becomes undeniable. The enemy will no longer pursue you, but will flee at the sound of your voice. When you appear, they will disappear because of the anointing of prayer that rests on you. Glory to God!

THE CHURCH NEEDS YOUR PRAYERS

Prayer for Your Local Church

One of the greatest responsibilities believers have is to pray for the body of Christ in their local community. When we consistently pray for our local Church, our hearts begin to align with the Lord's heart for His people. This connection does not remain confined to just the building or group of people we see weekly. Instead, through prayer, the Holy Spirit expands our vision to see

God's plan for the Church in our city, our region, our nation, and ultimately, the world.

1. The Importance of Fervent Prayer for the Church

The Church is the living Body of Christ on earth. As believers, we are called to uphold this body in prayer. The local Church, where we worship and fellowship, is crucial to God's plan. Through the Church, souls are won to the kingdom, believers are discipled, and the gospel is spread.

Praying for the Church is not an occasional task but a constant responsibility. The Apostle Paul, in his letters, often mentioned how he continually prayed for the Church in various cities (Ephesians 1: 16, Philippians 1: 3-4). He understood that the strength of the Church was directly related to the prayers of the saints. Likewise, we are called to pray fervently, with passion and persistence, for our local Church.

Just as Paul said in Colossians 4: 2, *"Devote yourselves to prayer, being watchful and thankful,"* we, too, must be vigilant in prayer. A Church that prays is a Church that grows. It becomes a place where the Spirit of God moves freely, and the enemy's plans are thwarted. The prayers we offer for our Church can open the door to revival, healing, and breakthroughs.

2. Aligning Our Hearts with God's Heart

When we pray for our local Church, we are not merely asking God to meet needs or solve problems; we are inviting Him to do a transformative work in our midst. Prayer opens our eyes to see the Church from God's perspective. Often, we come with our own expectations or frustrations about the Church, but through prayer, the Lord reshapes our view, helping us to understand His desires for the assembly.

As we persist in prayer, our hearts begin to feel what the Lord feels for His Church. He desires the Church to be a place of refuge, healing, and spiritual growth. When we pray in line with God's will, we begin to experience a deep connection, not only with Him but also with the vision He has for our local congregation.

In praying for the Church, our personal concerns fade into the background as we take on the greater burden of the Church's spiritual health. We start to see that our local assembly is not just an isolated group, but part of a much larger movement of God's people across regions, nations, and the world. God's plan for the Church is global, and He invites us to partner with Him through prayer.

3. The Ripple Effect of Local Church Prayer

When we commit to praying for our local Church, we are setting into motion a ripple effect that can impact far beyond our immediate assembly. The prayers we lift up for our Church can touch the wider body of Christ. As we pray for unity, growth, and spiritual maturity within our local congregation, God can use those prayers to influence other churches in the city, the region, and even the nation.

Prayer has no boundaries. While we may begin by praying for the needs and growth of our local Church, the Holy Spirit often expands our prayers to include other churches in our city and beyond. This is because the Church is one body, though many parts. What affects one part of the body affects the whole (1 Corinthians 12:12-14). Our prayers for revival in our local Church can contribute to a revival in the entire region.

4. The Global Perspective

As our prayer life deepens, the Holy Spirit broadens our understanding of God's global plan for His Church. Praying for our local Church is not disconnected from praying for the global Church. Each congregation, no matter how small or large, is part of the greater mission to make disciples of all nations (Matthew 28:19). By praying for our local Church, we are contributing to this mission.

The local Church is the heartbeat of the global Church. As we intercede for the Church in our community, we should also remember that we are connected to believers all over the world who are serving the same God, worshipping the same Savior, and advancing the same Kingdom. This is why Paul urged the believers to pray "*for all the saints*" (Ephesians 6:18). Our prayers for the local Church help to strengthen the entire body of Christ.

So, praying for your local Church should be a regular and essential part of your prayer life. It builds unity, strengthens the body, and aligns us with God's vision for His people. As we dedicate ourselves to this sacred responsibility, we can trust that the Lord will move powerfully in our midst, bringing transformation not only to our local congregation but also to the Church at large.

Pray for Your Pastors

As believers, we are called to pray for various aspects of our lives and the world around us. Among the most crucial prayer responsibilities is interceding for our pastors and church leaders. They face unique spiritual, emotional, and physical challenges as they guide us in our faith journey. Through prayer, we offer them strength and protection to fulfil their God-given calling.

Pray for Protection and Strength

One of the primary reasons to pray for your pastor is to cover them in God's protection. Just as Jesus asked Peter, James, and John to pray with Him in the Garden of Gethsemane, your pastor needs prayer support. Spiritual leaders, like the Apostle Paul, have always faced opposition from both external forces and internal challenges within the Church. Paul encountered resistance from "unbelievers" and conflict with *"brethren,"* and your pastor experiences similar struggles.

When the enemy wants to hinder the growth of the Church, he often targets the leadership. This opposition may come from individuals within the community or even from within the congregation itself. Division, strife, and misunderstanding can all become tools of the enemy to disrupt a church's unity and progress. By interceding for your pastor, you play a vital role in ensuring that he is shielded from these snares and traps.

Include in your prayers that God would guard him against people with impure motives, and ask the Lord to give him wisdom and discernment to navigate difficult situations. A pastor cannot fulfil all his duties in his own; he needs divine protection and your consistent intercession.

Pray for Clarity and Wisdom

Every pastor carries the responsibility of shepherding God's people. From preparing sermons to counselling individuals, organizing outreach programs, and managing church administration, pastors face an immense workload. On top of these daily duties, they are often faced with questions and concerns that require immediate answers and wisdom.

Like the Apostle Paul, who sought God's guidance in every decision, your pastor needs the wisdom to handle the many challenges he faces. In 2 Corinthians 1:11, Paul himself requested prayer from the believers for his ministry to succeed. Similarly, your pastor needs divine guidance to make decisions aligned with God's will, to lead the church effectively, and to address the spiritual and practical needs of the congregation.

When you pray, ask God to fill your pastor with the wisdom necessary to discern the right path in every situation. Pray for him to remain sensitive to the Holy Spirit's leading, allowing him to make decisions that glorify God and benefit the church. Your prayers can significantly impact his ability to follow God's will, and successfully lead the congregation.

Pray for Joy

The pastoral calling is beautiful and fulfilling but it often comes with its own set of responsibilities.

Paul, who faced many hardships in ministry, still maintained his joy in Christ, writing in Philippians 4:4, *"Rejoice in the Lord always."*

Your pastor counsels broken marriages, organizes mission outreaches, preaches every Sunday, and manages a myriad of other duties behind the scenes. When people he has invested in turn away or are ungrateful, it can be disheartening. The weight of these experiences can sap his energy and joy if not sustained by prayer.

Pray that your pastor will retain his joy.

Joy is the fuel that keeps a leader moving forward despite obstacles. Ask the Lord to help him find fulfilment in Christ. Your prayers can support him in holding on to the joy of the Lord, which is his strength (Nehemiah 8:10).

Pray for Spiritual Sensitivity and God's Will

In Colossians 4:2-3, Paul said to the church *"Continue in prayer, and watch in the same with thanksgiving; Withal praying also for us, that God would open unto us a door of utterance, to speak the mystery of Christ…"* Pastors today share the same desire to stay in the will of God and effectively communicate His Word.

As you pray for your pastor, ask God to keep him sensitive to the Holy Spirit. Pray that he will be led by God in everything, avoiding distractions or pitfalls. His ability to remain in alignment with God's will is crucial not only for his life but for the well-being of the entire congregation. When he is attuned to God's voice, the entire church will flourish under his leadership.

Pray that he continues to pursue God's will for himself, his family, and the church. A pastor must juggle the responsibility of ministry with family life, and both areas need prayerful attention. Ask God to bless his home and keep his family in unity, strength, and protection.

The Power of Intercession on Behalf of Pastors

When you lift your pastor up in prayer, you are actively supporting the spiritual well-being of the entire church. Your intercession is a powerful tool that can make a difference in your pastor's ministry and in the church's progress. Just as Aaron and Hur held up Moses' hands during the battle (Exodus 17: 12), your prayers can uplift your pastor, enabling him to lead with wisdom, joy, and divine strength.

By praying regularly for your pastor, you become a key contributor to the church's health and the advancement of God's Kingdom. In return, God promises blessings as you align yourself with His purpose, standing in the gap for His servants. Pray persistently, for in doing so, you hold the entire assembly before God and invite His power to move in ways beyond human understanding.

Matthew 10: 41 *"He that receiveth a prophet in the name of a prophet shall receive a prophet's reward; and he that receiveth a righteous man in the name of a righteous man shall receive a righteous man's reward."*

See the Church as God's Solution for Your City

Throughout the New Testament, prayers often centred on the Church, which God has established as a beacon of hope and a source of His solutions for the world. This shows God's vision for the Church as the answer to the challenges facing society.

The health and strength of the Church directly influence the well-being of communities, cities, and nations. When the Church rises in love, unity, and power, it becomes an agent of transformation, radiating God's grace and mercy to a world in need.

The Church is not just a gathering of believers; it is the embodiment of God's presence in the community, a place where healing, reconciliation, and restoration happen. When we lift the Church in prayer, we invite God to work through His people, igniting change that can reshape families, communities, and generations. Our prayers for the Church are prayers for the world.

Interceding for Vulnerable Children

One of the Church's most essential roles is to care for the vulnerable; those who are fatherless, motherless, and in need of guidance and support. In today's society, so many children are growing up without a strong parental presence. This gap often leads to brokenness, instability, and a search for belonging. Through prayer, we ask God to reach these children and fill the void in their lives with His love and comfort. We pray for fathers to rise up and take responsibility, leading and nurturing their children with the knowledge of God.

For the motherless, we pray that God would provide them with nurturing figures, mothers in the faith who are equipped with love, patience, and wisdom. The Church is called to model a *"pure and undefiled religion"* (James 1:27), demonstrating a compassion that reaches beyond our walls to care for those who have no one else. In doing so, we reflect the very heart of God, who is "Father to the fatherless" (Psalm 68:5).

A Spirit of Adoption

As believers, we carry the Spirit of adoption, through whom we cry, *"Abba, Father"* (Romans 8:14-16). This Spirit not only secures our relationship with God but compels us to extend that sense of family to others. Let us pray that Christian families would open their hearts to welcome and nurture children in need. We ask that they would be moved with compassion, understanding that these young ones are precious in God's sight, and that they would continually demonstrate God's love.

The Church as a Place of Healing and Belonging

In our prayers, let us ask God to help the Church become a sanctuary for those seeking healing, a refuge for the broken-hearted, and a place where the lost find belonging. As we pray for the Church to embody this role, we are essentially praying for the transformation of our cities. Imagine communities where no child feels abandoned, no widow is left in isolation, and every soul finds a place where they are valued and loved. This vision can become a reality when we faithfully pray and step out in obedience, letting God use the Church as His hands and feet.

So, let us lift our voices to pray for a Church that is united in mission, compassionate in love, and unwavering in faith. In doing so, we pray for a world where God's love, truth, and hope flourish.

We need to pray for the lonely who have nobody, that God should bring them to Him. And for the lonely who have people around them but these people are so self-centred that they feel lonely anyway, that The Lord Jesus will fill them with His presence and connect them to a living church so that they can discover the Love of Jesus through the church.

- We need to pray for those who are believing God for a husband, for a wife, that God would have mercy and provide the right person in their lives.

- Some people prefer to raise dogs than to raise humans beings. We need to pray for them that the Lord would send enlightenment for deliverance from self-centeredness. Let the compassion of Christ spread in our cities, and countries.

- We need to pray for those who are deciding for abortion, that the Lord would touch their hearts to make right decisions.

- We need to pray for restoration of divided families, that God's original institution of families should continue and perversion should be abolished in Jesus' name.

- For those who have the will to help and the means are needed that God might provide for their needs to be able to assist others in Jesus Name.

For those who are in deep pain due to the homes in which they live; homes marked by dysfunction, conflict, and a lack of love; let us intercede that they might encounter Jesus, the Prince of Peace, Who alone can bring lasting harmony and restoration. These families may struggle because they lack knowledge of the true source of peace, but through prayer, we can ask that they come to know Jesus as their comforter and guide. As they embrace Him, may their families be transformed into sanctuaries of safety and warmth, places where love and understanding replace strife and confusion.

We are called to lift up the sick in body, mind, and spirit. Many suffer from ailments that go beyond the physical, they carry emotional and spiritual wounds that need the touch of God's healing Hand. Let us bring these individuals before God, praying earnestly for their complete healing and deliverance in the powerful name of Jesus Christ. May they experience restoration not only in their bodies but in their hearts and souls, as they come to know God as their ultimate Healer, finding peace and wholeness in His presence.

In our prayers, let us also remember those who are homeless, abandoned, and forgotten by society. Many are suffering in silence, longing for someone to see them and offer a hand of compassion. Let us ask God to raise up a movement to restore these individuals, to lift them out of despair, and to establish them according to His perfect will. May the Lord not only wipe away their tears but also bless them abundantly, providing shelter, community, and a renewed sense of purpose. Let our prayers create pathways for them to encounter God's love in a profound way.

We need to pray earnestly that our God would multiply faithful watchmen and watchwomen in our cities; men and women of prayer who are vigilant, who stand in the gap for their communities. As these intercessors rise up, may our prayers extend over our cities, reaching the regions and nations, inviting God's leadership to prevail. May these watchmen be filled with discernment, courage, and a sense of purpose, and may they build walls of prayer around their communities to protect and uplift them in God's truth.

Finally, let us pray that God will redeem our time and give us the Spirit of fervent prayer. In a world filled with distractions and temptations, may we overcome the lusts of the world and find ourselves fully committed to God's purposes. Let us ask for divine wisdom, justice, and favour, so that we may walk uprightly in a world that often strays from truth. As we seek His face, may God release a mighty revival upon the earth. A revival that shakes nations, transforms hearts, and ushers in the reality of His kingdom. We declare, "Let Your kingdom come, Lord, and Your will be done," as we pray in Jesus' name.

Prayer for Students and Youth

Ephesians 1: 17-21 *"That the God of our Lord Jesus Christ, the Father of glory, may give unto you the Spirit of wisdom and revelation in the knowledge of Him: The eyes of your understanding being enlightened; that ye may know what is the hope of His calling, and what are the riches of the glory of His inheritance in the saints, And what is the exceeding greatness of His power to usward who believe, according to the working of His mighty power, Which He wrought in Christ, when He raised Him from the dead, and set Him at His own right hand in the heavenly places, Far above all principality, and power, and might, and dominion, and every name that is named, not only in this world, but also in that which is to come:"*

When praying for the youth, our intercession must be intentional, recognizing the immense challenges they face and the great potential they have as vessels for God's Kingdom. We need to pray specifically for breakthroughs in their lives, asking God to deliver them from fears, from worldly distractions, and from the traps of lust and other temptations that seek to derail their purpose.

Many young people are searching for fulfilment and identity, often looking in places that leave them feeling empty. As we lift them up in prayer, we ask God to reveal Himself powerfully to them, allowing them to experience the true joy and peace that only He can provide.

Our prayers should include a petition for the revelation of Jesus Christ among young people, praying for encounters that will transform their lives.

We believe the youth need God now more than ever, and with His touch, they can become dynamic instruments in the Kingdom: worshippers, intercessors, musicians, preachers, teachers, missionaries, and so much more. Let us pray that the Holy Spirit would increase His work in their hearts, giving them a hunger for God's Word and a passion to serve. We intercede for them to receive an outpouring of divine purpose, empowering them to step boldly into roles where they glorify God with their unique gifts and talents.

It is essential that we also pray for the Lord to apprehend their hearts, capturing their attention and redirecting their focus from the fleeting attractions of this world. We ask that God would grant them divine dreams, visions, visitations, and revelations that ground them in their faith and remind them of their calling. May God open their eyes to His beauty, helping them to see themselves as His beloved children, created for great purposes.

Our prayers must also include petitions for their protection. Young people are bombarded with influences that attempt to lure them away from God, but we trust in the power of prayer to safeguard their hearts and minds. We need to pray that they are guided by the Holy Spirit to make wise decisions, avoiding relationships and environments that could lead them astray. Let us pray that God raises up a generation of young people who, like David, are deeply devoted to God's heart, and like Daniel, refuse to defile themselves with the filth of this world. May they be resilient, able to resist peer pressure, and remain firm in their faith even when it's difficult.

In our intercession, we ask God to deliver them from all sexual immorality and lust. We pray for purity and a renewed commitment to holiness, asking that God create in them clean hearts and help them to be examples of righteousness among their peers. Our prayer is that they will choose the path of integrity, not swayed by the trends and patterns of the world but transformed by the renewing of their minds. May they find their strength in Christ and encourage one another in a pursuit of holiness, building each other up as a community set apart for God.

Pray for the Salvation of the Unbelievers

A strong, vibrant Church in your city acts as a beacon of hope and light, becoming a powerful instrument for transforming lives and confronting the darkness in the city. God desires to address the wickedness, sin, and spiritual blindness that hold so many captive. He has chosen the prayers of His people, especially through local Churches, to bring about this transformation. When the Church rises up in fervent prayer and unity, it paves the way for God to reveal His love, His truth, and His power over the evil forces.

Our role, then, is to intercede passionately for the conversion of those entangled in practices and organizations rooted in darkness, such as satanism, freemasonry, the illuminati, witchcraft, and various occult powers. God's love extends to every soul, and through our prayers, we can call them into the light of salvation. Just as God radically transformed Saul, a zealous persecutor of Christians into Paul, a devout apostle and ambassador of Christ, so too can He redeem and restore those currently deceived by darkness. We pray that, just as with Paul, the light of Christ would shine upon them, that they would encounter a life-changing revelation of Jesus. That the scales of spiritual blindness would fall from their eyes. Let them see the truth of God's love and His salvation, breaking free from the chains of spiritual captivity, in Jesus' Name.

Additionally, it is essential to pray against the destructive spirit of division, particularly racism and discrimination, which too often infiltrate the Church. When a person of one race feels unwelcome or uncomfortable around another in God's House, it hinders the unity that Christ called us to embody. We pray that the Lord would bring His Spirit of unity and love into our congregations, that all believers, regardless of race or background, would be united together in one faith, one hope, and one baptism. Let every Church be a place of true oneness in Christ, where divisions are dismantled, and believers see one another as brothers and sisters, equally loved and valued by God.

In a city with such a Church committed to interceding for the lost, standing firm against darkness, and united in Christ; we will see revival, salvation, and true transformation take place. Through the power of prayer, let our cities be places where the Kingdom of God advances, bringing light and freedom to every soul.

Pray for the Entire Church in Your City

The Church is a unified body composed of various congregations, ministries, and groups, each with its unique strengths, callings, and purposes. Yet, in prayer, our hearts should be set on seeking the Lord's desire for His Church as a whole; not only for individual congregations but for the entire body of believers within our cities and regions. The Lord's vision is not restricted to blessing one part of His body; He seeks to move powerfully across every gathering, every place where His name is lifted, and every believer who seeks His face.

Our prayer, then, is to align with His heart to see His Spirit poured out over every assembly and community within the Church, bringing revival, unity, and transformation. It's easy to focus on what God is doing in our immediate circles, but His desire is far greater. He longs to visit, transform, and empower the entire Church in a region; so that His light shines brightly in every corner of our cities.

When we pray, let us ask God not only to bless our own gatherings but to release a wave of His Spirit that renews and strengthens His people citywide, creating a Church that is vibrant, unified, and wholly surrendered to His will. In doing so, we become partners with Him in the greater mission for a Church that not only grows in number but also in love, power, and purpose, establishing His Kingdom here on earth.

Ask the Holy Spirit for Revelation

As you intercede for the Church in your area, invite the Holy Spirit to reveal His heart and desires for growth and transformation. Begin by asking the Holy Spirit to reveal what He feels about the Church; the strengths, the challenges, and the needs of the people. Take time to listen deeply, attuning your heart to receive insights, impressions, and words from the Lord. Allow these revelations to shape your prayers, directing them with a specific purpose and alignment with God's vision for His Church.

Our goal in prayer is not merely to offer words or petitions in a detached manner but to cultivate a growing sensitivity to what is in the Heart of the Lord. We are called to carry the Heart of Jesus for His Church, embracing both His compassion and His righteous desires. Over time, this practice will nurture in us a deep connection with God's will, guiding us to pray not just with words, but with His own Heart.

When we pray with this level of intimacy and agreement, our prayers become more powerful. They move from general petitions to focused, Spirit-led intercessions that strike directly at the needs and purposes God has identified. With this depth of partnership, prayer becomes a driving force for real, tangible changes within the Church and the community. We are empowered to do more than just intercede from afar; we are stirred to take action, to encourage, to serve, and to participate in God's vision. Ultimately advancing the Church's reach and impact within the entire area.

Positive Prayers for the Church

As believers, we must commit to always lifting up positive prayers for the Church and for our fellow believers. In times of burden and distress, it is essential to focus not on the negative aspects of situations but rather to seek the impartation of positive attributes and outcomes. When faced with challenges, our prayers should reflect hope, healing, and divine intervention.

While it is true that crises can, and do occur within the Church, our response should not be to dwell on the problems but to pray fervently for the impartation of good things. God desires that we approach our prayers with hearts that are fully awake and aware of the needs of the Church. This mindfulness enables us to focus on the blessings we seek to manifest, rather than the darkness we wish to avoid.

During prayer meetings, the atmosphere should be one of encouragement and positivity. Negative prayers can quickly drain the joy from a gathering, leading to an unproductive spirit of strife and division within the Church community. Instead, we must bring an environment where prayer uplifts, inspires, and unites believers in a common purpose.

Furthermore, it is crucial to remember that we are called to love and support one another, rather than criticize or condemn. When we slip into a pattern of negative prayers, we risk adopting an attitude of superiority or pride over fellow believers whom we perceive to be faltering in their faith. This is not the heart of Christ. Instead, let us choose to intercede on their behalf, asking God to extend His mercy and grace, enabling all of us to grow in love and faith.

Additionally, we should approach those who seem to be struggling, encouraging them gently to turn back to God. Our role is not to judge but to restore, to uplift, and to bring about reconciliation within the body of Christ. By cultivating a habit of positive prayers, we align ourselves with God's Heart for His Church, promoting an atmosphere of love, grace, and unity.

Pray for Revelation to Fulfil Our Calling

In Ephesians 1: 17-19, we are invited into a profound understanding of our relationship with the Father of Glory. The Apostle Paul prays that God may bestow upon us the Spirit of wisdom and revelation, enabling us to truly know Him. This knowledge goes beyond mere intellectual understanding; it speaks to an experiential, heart-deep comprehension of who God is and His purposes for our lives.

Paul emphasizes the importance of having our eyes enlightened, allowing us to perceive the divine truths that often remain obscured in our day-to-day existence. Through prayer, we seek this enlightenment, asking the Holy Spirit to illuminate our hearts and minds so we can grasp the richness of our faith. This enlightenment leads us to a deeper understanding of the hope to which we are called. It assures us of God's specific calling on our lives, providing clarity and direction amid the chaos of our circumstances.

Moreover, Paul reminds us of the incredible inheritance we possess as saints in Christ. This inheritance is not merely a future promise; it is in our present reality as beloved children of God. Understanding the magnitude of our inheritance brings us a sense of belonging and purpose, revealing our destiny as children of God.

Finally, apostle Paul speaks of the exceeding greatness of God's power directed toward us who believe. This power is not passive; it is active, dynamic, and transformative. It reflects the very Might of God at work in our lives, enabling us to overcome challenges and fulfilling His plans for us. As we engage in prayer, we tap into this divine power, empowering us to live out our calling with boldness and confidence.

In essence, this passage is a prayer for enlightenment, understanding, and empowerment, urging us to lean into the depths of God's wisdom and grace. It challenges us to pursue a relationship with God that transcends surface-level engagement and invites us into a transformative journey of discovery, assurance, and divine capability.

Pray for the Power of the Holy Spirit and the Presence of Jesus in You Personally

Ephesians 3:16-19 states, "*[16] That He would grant you, according to the riches of His glory, to be strengthened with might by His Spirit in the inner man; [17] That Christ may dwell in your hearts by faith; that ye, being rooted and grounded in love, [18] May be able to comprehend with all saints what is the breadth, and length, and depth, and height; [19] And to know the love of Christ, which passeth knowledge, that ye might be filled with all the fulness of God.*"

In this profound passage, the Apostle Paul expresses a deep prayer for the believers in Ephesus, and indeed for all of us, emphasizing the immeasurable resources of God's glory available to those who seek Him. He starts with a request for divine strength, a strength that transcends mere human ability, bestowed through the Holy Spirit. This inner fortitude empowers us to face life's challenges, transforming our spiritual lives from within. As we invite the Spirit to strengthen us, we cultivate a deeper relationship with God, allowing Christ to dwell richly in our hearts.

This indwelling of Christ is not a passive presence but an active manifestation of His love and grace within us. It requires faith; a trust that goes beyond understanding and into the realm of spiritual experience. Rooted and grounded in love, we are called to develop a foundation that is unwavering, ensuring that our lives reflect the love of Christ in every interaction.

Apostle Paul urges us to comprehend the vastness of Christ's love. The dimensions he describes are the width, length, depth, and height, this serves as metaphors for a love that knows no bounds. This is not just an intellectual acknowledgment of Christ's love; it is an invitation to experience it fully. Through our connection with other believers, we can grasp the immeasurable love of Christ, which surpasses all human comprehension. This communal aspect of faith encourages us to share in one another's experiences, deepening our understanding of God's love.

Finally, Paul culminates this prayer with a desire for us to be filled with all the fullness of God. This fullness encompasses His attributes: His grace, mercy, power, and love; transforming us into vessels that reflect His character. As we engage in fervent prayer, seeking to align our hearts with His, we invite the fullness of God into our lives, enabling us to be effective witnesses of His glory and people of His love in the world.

Pray for God's Love to Abound in You Through Righteous Living

In Philippians 1:9-11, the Apostle Paul expresses a profound prayer for the believers, which resonates deeply with our journey of faith:

"And this I pray, that your love may abound yet more and more in knowledge and in all judgment; [10] *That ye may approve things that are excellent; that ye may be sincere and without offence till the day of Christ.* [11] *Being filled with the fruits of righteousness, which are by Jesus Christ, unto the glory and praise of God."*

This passage invites us to consider the transformative power of love; a love that is not merely emotional but is rooted in knowledge and discernment of God's character and ways. Apostle Paul emphasizes that our love should grow abundantly, suggesting an ongoing, dynamic relationship with God that enriches our understanding and enhances our capacity to discern His will.

When we seek the knowledge of God, we are not just accumulating facts; we are engaging in a deep relational experience that enables us to see the world through His eyes. This divine perspective equips us to make choices that align with His heart, leading us to rejoice in what is excellent and valuable. In a world filled with distractions and compromises, this discernment allows us to remain sincere; genuine in our faith and actions; avoiding offense not just in our relationships with others but also in our relationship with Christ.

Moreover, being "filled with the fruits of righteousness" speaks to the tangible outcomes of our relationship with God. These attributes of the fruit of the Spirit: love, joy, peace, patience, kindness, goodness, faithfulness, gentleness, and self-control, are not merely abstract concepts but the evidence of a life transformed by prayer and divine interaction. They reflect the holiness that God calls us to pursue, a holiness that is marked by integrity.

As we pray for our love to abound in discernment, we must also recognize the ultimate purpose of this growth: the glory and praise of God. Our lives, when lived in this fullness, become testimonies of His grace and power, drawing others to Him and expanding His kingdom. This passage invites us into a deeper understanding of prayer as a vital practice that cultivates our hearts and minds, equipping us to navigate life with wisdom, sincerity, and a commitment to holiness.

Pray to Know God's Will, to Be Fruitful in Ministry and Strengthened by Intimacy with God

In Colossians 1:9-11, the Apostle Paul prays deeply for the believers, not only asking that they be filled with knowledge but specifically with *"the knowledge of His will."* This is a profound call for believers to understand God's intentions, desires, and plans with clarity, grounded in *"all wisdom and spiritual understanding."* Such wisdom is not merely intellectual; it is wisdom birthed from God's Spirit, enabling believers to perceive things from a divine perspective, to discern what truly matters, and to understand the heart of God.

When we are filled with this kind of spiritual knowledge, our lives are transformed into a walk that is *"worthy of the Lord,"* one that reflects His character and fulfils His purpose. A life pleasing to God is not passive but active, marked by fruitfulness in every good work. This fruitfulness is the natural outpouring of an intimate relationship with God, bearing witness to His transformative power within us. It is a journey of growing deeper in the knowledge of God, a continual pursuit where we understand Him more, and are conformed to His image.

Moreover, this passage calls for strength; the strength that comes from God's *"glorious power."* This is not a human strength that wanes but a divine empowerment, an inner might that enables believers to walk with patience and perseverance fully trusting in God's sovereignty and faithfulness.

As we incorporate Paul's prayer into our lives, we too seek to be filled with divine wisdom, to walk in ways that honour God, and to be strengthened by His power so we may face every season with patience, perseverance, and joy. This prayer becomes a blueprint for us to model our prayers for others and a reminder of God's desire for us to be fruitful, resilient, and spiritually enriched in every way.

Pray for Unity in the Church and to Be Filled with Supernatural Joy, Peace, Hope and Confidence

Romans 15: 5-6 is a Prayer for Unity, Hope, and Joy in the Holy Spirit

"Now may the God of patience and comfort grant you to be like-minded toward one another, according to Christ Jesus, that you may with one mind and one mouth glorify the God and Father of our Lord Jesus Christ."

Here, Paul prays that God, the source of patience and comfort, will enable His followers to walk in *unity and mutual understanding*. In a world filled with divisions, this prayer serves as a reminder that true unity is found not in uniformity, but in aligning our hearts and minds with the heart of Christ. To be "like-minded" is to set aside personal agendas, selfish ambitions, and pride, and instead, seek the mind of Christ, who, even as Lord, humbly served others. When believers are united in purpose and spirit, God is glorified, and our collective worship becomes a powerful testimony.

The prayer for unity is not just about agreement, but about cultivating a spirit of love and acceptance, rooted in Christ's example. In this way, the Church is strengthened, and we can be "with one mind and one mouth," glorifying God together. This unified worship honours the Father and reveals His love to those who witness it.

Romans 15: 13 *"Now may the God of hope fill you with all joy and peace in believing, that you may abound in hope by the power of the Holy Spirit."*

Apostle Paul continues by emphasizing the role of God as the source of hope, filling our hearts with joy and peace. It is this hope that sustains us. It is not a hope rooted in our circumstances, but a divine hope that surpasses understanding; a hope that strengthens our faith and enables us to trust God's promises.

Joy and peace are the fruits of trusting God, and they spring forth as we deepen our belief in Him. When we open our hearts fully to the Holy Spirit, we experience a supernatural hope that lifts us beyond the limits of our natural understanding and abilities. It is through this hope, given by the power of the Holy Spirit, that we are empowered to face each day with courage and a sense of purpose.

May we, as believers, pray for this same hope, joy, and peace to fill our lives so that we may reflect Christ's light to those around us. As we embrace this prayer, let us become vessels of God's hope and peace, and share His love with the world.

Pray to Be Enriched by the Gifts of the Holy Spirit

1 Corinthians 1: 5-8 paints a beautiful picture of how believers are enriched by God's grace in every way, empowered for the purposes of His kingdom. This divine enrichment touches every

area of life, strengthening us in both *"utterance"* and *"knowledge."* Through anointed preaching, inspired singing, and Spirit-filled speech, we are given the ability to share the gospel message with power and effectiveness, reaching hearts and minds in ways that go beyond our natural capacities.

In addition to utterance, Paul speaks of *"all knowledge"*; an insight that transcends earthly understanding, rooted in prophetic revelation. This is not mere intellectual knowledge but a deeper awareness birthed from our relationship with God. It's a form of divine wisdom that comes through prayer, intimacy with the Holy Spirit, and time in His Word. By receiving this kind of knowledge, we are enabled to discern God's purposes and plans for ourselves and others, and to act in alignment with His will.

The *"testimony of Christ"* is also confirmed in us through miracles, signs, and wonders, testifying to the truth of Jesus and His resurrection. Miracles serve as a living testimony of Christ's presence and power among us, inspiring others to believe and reaffirming our own faith. In this way, the Holy Spirit ensures we have what we need to serve God effectively. Our gifts, whether in prophecy, teaching, healing, or serving, are tools to build up the body of Christ as we eagerly anticipate His return.

Furthermore, Paul assures us that Christ will *"confirm"* us to the end, ensuring that we remain steadfast, unmovable, and faithful to His calling. This divine confirmation is not a one-time event; it is an ongoing process of being held, guided, and strengthened by God's power. We are reassured that as we walk in faith and rely on His strength, He will keep us blameless until the day of our Lord's return.

Ultimately, these verses remind us that God's provision and empowerment are continuous. By enriching us in all utterance, all knowledge, and all gifts, He prepares us for His work and sustains us as we look forward to the fullness of His kingdom. Our journey is safeguarded by the One who began this work in us and will bring it to completion, securing our place in His eternal family.

Pray for the Release of Grace to Bring the Church to Maturity and Holiness

1 Thessalonians 3:10-13 gives us a powerful model for intercessory prayer, showing how prayer can be a tool in shaping and strengthening our faith and love. Paul writes, "*Praying exceedingly that... (God will release His Spirit and grace to) perfect what is lacking in your faith... And may the Lord make you increase and abound in love to one another and to all... that He may establish your hearts blameless in holiness before our God and Father.*"

This prayer reveals the dual nature of a believer's growth in God: strengthening our faith and cultivating love. Paul intercedes for the Thessalonian church, desiring that God fills any gaps in their understanding and faith, knowing that only by God's Spirit can believers reach maturity. This type of prayer reminds us that our faith journey is not a solitary effort but a partnership with God and those who pray for us.

The prayer continues, showing that an increase in love is essential to living in alignment with God's heart. Apostle Paul prays that their love would not merely be adequate, but would overflow;

abounding toward each other and extending to everyone. This love is a mark of spiritual maturity that signifies God's transformative work within us.

Finally, Paul's prayer seeks for the believers' hearts to be "*established... blameless in holiness.*" Holiness here is not merely outward righteousness but a deep inner alignment with God's character. This prayer thus becomes a blueprint: we pray that God's Spirit perfects our faith, enriches us in love, and makes us steadfast in holiness. When we intercede for others, we're asking God to bring about this transformation, producing believers who are both grounded in faith and radiant in love.

Pray to Be Worthy to Walk in the Fullness of Your Destiny in God

2 Thessalonians 1:11-12 gives us a powerful example of intercessory prayer that is purposeful and deeply encouraging. The Apostle Paul says, "*Therefore we also pray always for you that our God would count you worthy of this* **calling, and** *fulfill all the good pleasure of His* **goodness and the work of faith with power,** *¹²that the name of our Lord Jesus Christ may be glorified in you, and you in Him, according to the grace of our God and the Lord Jesus Christ.*"

This prayer reveals God's desire for His children to live lives that are worthy of their divine calling; a calling not based on our strength but on His gracious purpose.

Firstly, he prays that we might be "*counted worthy*" of our calling. This worthiness is not about personal merit; rather, it's a reminder to live in a way that honours the incredible gift of grace we've received. To be *"counted worthy"* is to allow God to shape our character so we become vessels that reflect His holiness and love. Such worthiness is a result of yielding to His Spirit, allowing our lives to be transformed and aligned with His desires.

Secondly, Paul prays that God would fulfil all the *"good pleasure of His goodness."* This speaks of God's generous intentions and purposes for us, which include plans for our spiritual growth, empowerment, and effective service in His kingdom. Paul's choice of the words *"good pleasure"* signifies the delight God takes in blessing and equipping us for every good work. When we walk in alignment with His plans, we not only fulfil our purpose but also experience a deep joy and satisfaction that can only come from knowing we are in His will.

Lastly, Paul prays for the *"work of faith with power."* Faith, when acted upon, requires divine empowerment. God's power enables us to carry out our mission with effectiveness and impact that go beyond human ability. Paul's prayer reminds us that we are to step out in faith, trusting in God's might to strengthen and sustain our efforts. Every act of faith, whether small or large, is backed by the authority and power of God Himself.

The ultimate goal of this prayer is *"that the name of Jesus may be glorified in you, and you in Him."* As we walk in worthiness, submit to His plans, and allow faith to be empowered by His Spirit, our lives bring honour to our Lord Jesus. And in turn, we share in His glory; reflecting His light, wisdom, and power to the world.

This prayer becomes a pattern for our intercession for others, a way of supporting them to fulfil their divine calling and receive strength, guidance, and empowerment from God. It reminds us that all we do is by His grace and for His glory, urging us to press into prayer with even greater fervour.

Pray that the Word of God Will Increase in Influence and Effectiveness as God Releases His Power on It

In 2 Thessalonians 3:1-5, Paul asks the church: *"pray for us, that the Word of the Lord may run swiftly* (rapidly increase its influence) *and be glorified* (confirmed with apostolic power and miracles), *just as it is with you."* This request reveals Paul's deep reliance on prayer for the success of his mission. His words remind us that prayer is essential when we desire that God's Word might reach people's hearts with a powerful, life-transforming impact.

Paul's desire is for the Gospel to *"run swiftly"* is a metaphor for the unhindered spread of God's message. Just as an athlete runs freely on a clear path, Paul prays for the Word of God to advance rapidly without obstruction, cutting through cultural barriers, misunderstandings, and spiritual resistance. Here, we see the urgency of prayer for God's Word to break down obstacles and establish itself in new hearts and people. It's a prayer for the Gospel to reach those who have not yet encountered its life-giving truth, as well as for a deepening of understanding among those already following Christ.

He continues in verse 3; *"The Lord is faithful, Who will establish you and guard you from the evil one."* This portion speaks of God's promise to both strengthen and protect His people. Paul assures the church that as they pray, God Himself is actively involved in building their faith, making them steadfast and immovable in their convictions. This reminds us that prayer is not only a request for external outcomes but also a means of internal fortification. The faithful God is our Rock, guarding us from spiritual attacks and temptations that aim to weaken our walk with Him.

Finally, Paul concludes with a blessing: 5 *"May the Lord direct your hearts into the love of God and into the patience* (perseverance or endurance) *of Christ."* This prayer seeks more than just protection or power; it seeks transformation at the core of our being. To have our hearts directed into God's love means to dwell in a love that overcomes all fear, anxiety, and doubt. It's a call for believers to be so rooted in the experience of God's love that it becomes the driving force of their faith. Furthermore, Paul prays for the *"endurance of Christ"* in them; a resilience modelled by Jesus Himself, who faced suffering with unwavering commitment and joy for the sake of God's glory.

Through this passage, we are reminded that prayer is both a shield and a guiding light, leading us deeper into God's love and the perseverance that Christ exemplified. Let this inspire us to continually pray for one another, that the Word of the Lord may increase and be honoured in the world, transforming lives and bringing glory to God.

Pray for Impartation of Boldness in Speaking the Word by Releasing Healings, Signs and Wonders Following

In Acts 4: 29-31, we see a profound example of the Church's reliance on prayer to invite God's intervention and to empower their mission: *"Lord...grant to Your servants that with all boldness they may speak Your Word, by stretching out Your Hand to heal, and that signs and wonders may be done through the name of Your holy Servant Jesus. And when they had prayed, the place where they were assembled together was shaken; and they were all filled with the Holy Spirit, and they spoke the Word of God with boldness."*

The early Church found itself surrounded by threats, opposition, and the formidable task of spreading the Gospel message in a world that often responded with hostility. But rather than seeking safety or comfort, their prayer was for boldness; a boldness that would enable them to speak God's Word without fear. This prayer reveals their deep commitment to the mission, prioritizing the fulfilment of God's work over their own security. Their hearts were set on advancing His Kingdom, and they sought a supernatural strength to do so, asking God to extend His hand to heal and perform signs and wonders in Jesus' Name. Their prayer was not a plea to avoid trials; rather, it was a plea for God's manifest presence to be revealed through them.

In response to this prayer, God answered in a remarkable way: the physical space they occupied was shaken, a tangible sign of His power and approval. This moment serves as a vivid reminder that prayer is a powerful catalyst for divine action. The shaking of the room symbolizes God's readiness to move and the Holy Spirit's active presence, willing to embolden His people when they pray in faith and humility. They were filled anew with the Holy Spirit, equipping them with both the courage and clarity needed to proclaim the Word of God.

The outcome was unmistakable; these believers did not leave that room the same as when they entered. They were transformed and immediately began to speak God's Word with a fresh boldness. This passage emphasizes the pattern we see throughout the book of Acts: the Church, in its most vulnerable and uncertain moments, responded by gathering together in **prayer**. They called upon God with a unified voice, and He answered by empowering them to be witnesses, not through their own strength, but through the undeniable presence and power of the Holy Spirit.

For us today, this account challenges us to consider the focus of our own prayers. Are we seeking comfort, or are we willing to ask God for boldness to accomplish His will?

Acts 4:29-31 calls us to a higher level of prayer, one that seeks alignment with God's purposes and relies on His power rather than our own. It is a reminder that when we pray for the boldness to speak His Word, God will respond; He will fill us with His Spirit, shake the foundations of doubt and fear within us, and equip us to serve Him courageously in a world that desperately needs to witness His glory.

Pray for the Release of God's Promise to Empower You

In prayer, we wait on God not only for His answers but also for His empowerment. This promise to be *"endued with power"* is an invitation to those who patiently tarry, seeking God's presence with an open heart and a fervent spirit. As we pray, let us ask for a release of this divine strength upon every labourer; those who, day by day, engage in God's work, both in the Church and beyond.

Let our prayers echo the desire for God's Spirit to move in power, equipping His people with a holy boldness, resilience, and a supernatural strength to overcome the challenges and resistance they face. For all who tarry and persist in prayer, may we be granted breakthroughs that only the Spirit can bring, breakthroughs that will turn obstacles into opportunities and open doors to proclaim the Good News with authority and love. Amen!

Luke 24: 49 records the promise Jesus Christ gave to the disciples: "*Behold, I send the Promise of My Father upon you; but tarry in the city of Jerusalem until you are endued with power from on high.*" This power is not only for their personal lives but for the fulfilment of their calling, a calling that would ignite the spread of the gospel across the world.

This promise continues for us today, extending to each labourer in the Kingdom. Acts 1: 8 reiterates this with Jesus Christ' words, "*You shall receive power when the Holy Spirit has come upon you; and you shall be witnesses to Me in Jerusalem... and to the end of the earth.*" As we pray, let us ask for this Spirit-given power to flow through all who serve, from pastors and evangelists to every believer working to advance God's Kingdom.

Pray for the manifestation of this power in every area of service, for divine insight and anointing that only the Holy Spirit can impart. Let us believe for breakthroughs that will affirm God's presence and enable the Church to witness effectively, carrying His light to the ends of the earth.

Pray for the Lord's Presence to Destroy all Resistance

Let us pray for the Lord to release His zeal, a divine passion that burns like fire for His people, so that His manifest presence will descend with might, shaking and dismantling all forms of resistance. It is through His intense, Holy zeal that the obstacles opposing His people will crumble and be consumed, allowing His purposes to prevail. Our prayer should call upon His powerful, undeniable presence to come down in such a way that every force of opposition stands no chance, and every barrier is reduced to ashes before Him.

Isaiah's words capture this passionate plea for divine intervention: *"Oh, that You would rend the heavens! That You would come down, that the mountains might shake at Your presence—as fire burns brushwood, as fire causes water to boil—to make Your name known to Your adversaries, that the nations may tremble at Your presence!"* (Isaiah 64: 1-2).

These verses reflect a cry for God's power to be made so evident. Just as fire ignites dry brushwood or brings water to a boiling point, we ask the Lord to reveal His anointing in a way that even the most hardened hearts recognize His majesty. When the Lord intervenes, His name becomes known not only to His people but to His enemies as well, and every knee bows in awe of His holy presence.

"When You did awesome things for which we did not look (expect)... Since the beginning of the world men have not heard, nor has the eye seen any God besides You, Who acts for the one who waits for Him" (Isaiah 64: 3-4).

Isaiah reminds us that the Lord is a God Who acts, but not in ways we can always predict. Our prayers must reflect a surrender, allowing Him to act in His own time and in His own way, often beyond what we imagine. When we trust and wait on Him, He meets us in ways that are beyond human comprehension. The scripture declares that no one has ever seen, heard, or known a God like ours, who faithfully and powerfully acts on behalf of those who earnestly seek Him.

The Lord honours those who walk in His ways, who hold tightly to righteousness, and who seek Him with gladness and fervency. He meets them in their waiting and rewards their faithful prayers with His presence. So, let us seek His intervention, not only for personal victories but that His name would be lifted high, drawing all nations to tremble at His glory and all resistance to melt in His presence.

Pray for the Release of God's Promise: Dreams, Visions, and Prophecy in the Body of Christ

In Acts 2:17-21, God promises a powerful outpouring of His Spirit, a prophetic gift to believers that signifies the unfolding of His purpose in the last days: *"In the last days, says God, I will pour out of My Spirit on all flesh; your sons and your daughters shall prophesy, your young men shall see visions, your old men shall dream dreams…"* This divine promise to pour out His Spirit comes with a release of spiritual insight; dreams, visions, and prophecy which are meant to strengthen, guide, and embolden the Body of Christ to carry forward His work with clarity and conviction.

This prophecy is a call to intercession, urging us to pray fervently for its manifestation within our churches, families, and communities. When we pray for the release of God's Spirit, we position ourselves to receive a greater flow of divine revelation and wisdom, empowering the Body of Christ to fulfil the calling in these critical times. We should pray with expectation, asking for God's Spirit to awaken His people and ignite a fire within them to prophesy, to see His visions, and to dream dreams filled with His purpose.

The outpouring of the Spirit of God activates a level of spiritual awareness and insight that not only reveals God's plans but also prepares His people to respond effectively. Prophecy enables believers to speak God's Will into current situations, visions provide clarity and direction for the path ahead, and dreams become a vehicle for divine communication that speaks to the heart and spirit. This supernatural empowerment is not limited to pastors or leaders but is available to all believers, regardless of age, background, or position, as God's Spirit moves freely among His people.

This passage also gives us a sense of urgency: *"...I will show wonders in heaven above and signs in the earth beneath: blood, fire, and vapor of smoke. The sun shall be turned into darkness, and the moon into blood, before the coming of the great and awesome day of the Lord."* These signs remind us that we are in pivotal times, and the Body of Christ must be alert, spiritually awake, and ready for the fulfilment of God's plan. Praying for the outpouring of God's Spirit prepares the Church to navigate these times with wisdom, grace, and power.

Let us also remember the final promise in this passage: *"Whoever calls on the name of the Lord shall be saved."* Our intercession for the Spirit's outpouring is not just for revelation but for salvation; for a mighty move of repentance and renewal that will draw people from every background to the saving knowledge of Christ. In praying for the release of God's Spirit, we are not only interceding for the empowerment of believers, but also for the harvest of souls, that many may come to know Him through the signs and wonders that testify of His glory.

As you pray for the release of God's promise, ask the Holy Spirit to make this scripture a reality in our time. Seek Him to manifest His power through dreams, visions, and prophecy, so that His people may walk in step with His will and be instruments of His transformative power on the earth.

Pray for the Israel of God to be Saved and for the Release of Prophetic Anointing, Miracles, and Righteousness

In our prayers, we must earnestly seek the salvation of the Israel of God. The Apostle Paul expresses this profound desire in Romans 10:1, where he declares, "*My heart's desire and prayer to God for Israel is that they may be saved.*" This heartfelt longing should resonate within us as we intercede for Israel, recognizing the significance of the spiritual journey and our role in it.

The promise of salvation for Israel is reaffirmed in Romans 11:26-27 "*All Israel will be saved; the Deliverer will come out of Zion. He will turn away ungodliness from Jacob; for this is My covenant with them, when I take away their sins.*" Here, we see the hope of a divine intervention, a time when God's grace will be poured out upon His chosen people. We are reminded that God's faithfulness to His covenant endures, and through our prayers, we can facilitate the unfolding of this sacred promise.

Moreover, Isaiah 62:1 challenges us to be active participants in this divine mission: *"For Zion's sake, I will not hold My peace, and for Jerusalem's sake, I will not rest until her righteousness goes forth as brightness, and her salvation as a lamp that burns."* This verse emphasizes the urgency of our intercession, calling for a release of the prophetic Spirit that empowers us to speak God's truth into existence. We cannot remain silent or inactive; we must cry out for the release of miracles and the manifestation of righteousness in the land.

As we pray for the Israel of God, let us invoke the prophetic anointing to flow freely among His people. Pray for hearts to be softened, for eyes to be opened, and for the scales of disbelief to fall away. Let us ask for a fresh outpouring of the Holy Spirit, igniting a revival that brings forth signs and wonders, drawing many to the knowledge of Christ.

In this season of prayer, let our hearts align with God's heart for His people. May our intercessions be fervent and unwavering, standing in the gap until the day when all Israel shall be saved, and righteousness shines forth like the dawn. Let us boldly declare, in faith and expectation, the transformation that is to come.

Pray for the Anointing of Revival Fire to Fall in Your Assembly and in Your Whole Region

As you intercede, fervently pray for the anointing of revival fire to fall not only upon your assembly but also across your entire region. This prayer is a cry from the depths of your spirit, seeking an outpouring of God's transformative power that ignites hearts and revives the weary.

Revival is not just a momentary spark; it is a divine movement that breathes life into the dry bones of our communities. It is in this season of revival that the Name of Jesus can be lifted high, shining like a beacon of hope and salvation. The presence of God, manifested through revival, draws people to Him, transforming lives and hearts in profound ways.

Understand that this revival fire is ignited by the Spirit of God; it is His will to bring renewal and restoration to His people. When the anointing falls, chains are broken, the lost are found, and faith is rekindled. It stirs a passion within us, urging us to proclaim the Good News boldly and to demonstrate God's love through our actions.

Let us align our hearts with the desires of the Father and earnestly seek His presence. As we do, we will witness a mighty movement of God in our midst, a revival that not only impacts our assemblies but also spreads throughout our neighbourhoods, cities, and beyond.

The only way the name of Jesus can be lifted high is when there is revival. It is by the Spirit of God and it is the Will of God. Amen.

CHAPTER 2

WHAT HAPPENS WHEN YOU DO NOT PRAY?

WHAT HAPPENS WHEN YOU DO NOT PRAY?

When we engage in any form of prayer; whether intercession, thanksgiving, or worship the approach should be
with the understanding that we are stepping onto a spiritual bat-
tlefield. In this realm, two kingdoms are in constant opposition:
the Kingdom of God which is The Kingdom of light, truth, and
life, against the kingdom of darkness, characterized by deception, chaos, and evil.

Prayer is not just a dialogue with our Heavenly Father; it is a
divine weapon, an instrument in the hands of God's people,
equipped with the power to dismantle strongholds, break chains,
and usher in His will on earth as it is in heaven. As children of
God, we stand on the victorious side, clothed in the authority giv-
en to us through Christ. Yet, it is precisely because of this victory
and the potency of prayer that the forces of darkness wage war
relentlessly against our prayer lives, knowing well the damage a
praying believer can inflict upon their plans.

The enemy's tactics are subtle yet consistent; he knows that if he can hinder, distract, or discourage us, he can weaken our spiritual defences and rob us of the strength we gain in the presence of God. We are cautioned in Scripture to be vigilant and discerning, fully aware of the enemy's schemes. As he seeks to disrupt our communion with God, to sow seeds of doubt, complacency, and distraction, so that our prayers become half-hearted, our focus diluted, and our resolve weakened.

However, as believers, we are not ignorant of his strategies and devices. Scripture calls us to equip ourselves with the whole armour of God, covering ourselves in truth, righteousness, faith, salvation, and the Word of God. With these tools, we stand fortified against every tactic designed to weaken our spiritual focus and commitment.

It is crucial for Christians to recognize the various forms of spiritual interference that attempt to prevent effective prayer. These distractions may come in the form of busy schedules, unexpected interruptions, or a feeling of apathy toward spending time in prayer. While these interruptions may seem like ordinary, they often carry a deeper intention in the spiritual realm. Even subtle thoughts of doubt, impatience, or discouragement are arrows aimed at our minds, seeking to weaken our confidence in prayer. Recognizing these symptoms for what they are: spiritual weapons aimed at breaking our connection with God, is a vital step in resisting them. When we understand these signs, we can rise above them, standing firm and pressing deeper into prayer, knowing that each moment spent in God's presence is both a victory in the present battle and a preparation for those to come.

To persevere in prayer is to wield the power given to us through Christ, fully embracing our calling as intercessors, warriors, and beloved children of God. Let us, therefore, approach each prayer with readiness, intentionality and determination, understanding that, though the battle may be fierce, we fight from a place of victory, and through prayer, we bring heaven's reality into our lives, our society, and our world.

COMMON SPIRITUAL DISTRACTIONS

· Persistent Postponements: An Insidious Attack on our Spiritual Momentum

One of the most subtle yet effective tactics the enemy uses is the urge to delay prayer for reasons that may seem valid or even important. This sense of postponement can feel justified; like a need to address an urgent task, attend to a pressing matter, or wait for a "better" time to pray. However, these delays often become a repetitive cycle, subtly draining our spiritual momentum and weakening the resolve.

The more someone puts off prayer, the more challenging it becomes to return to it with the same intensity and passion. Over time, these small postponements accumulate, creating a growing distance between people and their intimate fellowship with God. It is crucial to recognize that these seemingly minor delays are not merely lapses in discipline but a calculated tactic of spiritual warfare. By persistently postponing prayer, the enemy seeks to wear down your resolve, leaving somebody spiritually drained and vulnerable.

Overcoming this trap requires an intentional commitment to prioritize prayer above all else, regardless of distractions or interruptions. Setting dedicated times for prayer and adhering to them as faithfully as any other appointment is essential. By confronting and resisting this tactic, we can maintain the spiritual momentum that fuels our walk with God, empowering us to remain steadfast, alert, and continually connected to His presence.

· Feelings of Uneasiness or Restlessness

At times, as you prepare to enter prayer, you may feel a sudden sense of discomfort, anxiety, or restlessness. This internal disturbance, often hard to ignore, can make it challenging to focus or settle into communion with God. These uneasy feelings may not simply be random distractions but could indicate a form of spiritual resistance. The enemy aims to disturb your minds, filling your hearts with doubt or anxiety to keep you from reaching a place of peace and intimacy with God. Recognizing these moments is crucial, as they often serve as signals of spiritual opposition working to distract you from prayer. Through such disruptions, the adversary hopes to divert your attention from the strength, joy, and clarity you receive when you connect with God. In these instances, you are reminded to be steadfast, calling on the Holy Spirit to empower you to press through, casting all your worries aside and focusing your hearts and minds fully on the Lord. By overcoming these obstacles, you draw closer to God, growing stronger in your faith and more resilient against spiritual interference.

· Unexpected Bodily Needs

In the midst of prayer, seemingly minor physical needs can suddenly appear urgent, subtly distracting you from your spiritual focus. It may be the sudden urge to go to the restroom, quench your thirst, grab a quick snack, or handle an "urgent" task that didn't seem pressing moments before. These needs often arise out of nowhere, shifting your attention away from prayer. Such distractions can serve as subtle, unassuming tactics that derail your connection with God, interrupting the flow of prayer and breaking the sacred atmosphere you're cultivating. While tending to your physical needs is important, it's essential to recognize when these distractions are simply attempts to pull you away from deeper communion with God. By staying aware of these subtle diversions and resisting the impulse to act immediately, you can maintain your focus, remain steadfast in prayer, and prioritize your spiritual needs over fleeting physical urges.

· Irritations or Anger Toward Prayer Leaders or Others Nearby

Feelings of irritation or anger toward those around you, such as church leaders, family members, or fellow believers, can often surface unexpectedly. These emotions can arise subtly, from seemingly minor frustrations or misunderstandings, yet they have the potential to create division and discord. When directed toward a prayer leader, for instance, these feelings can interrupt the flow of prayer and prevent the unity needed to intercede effectively. In the home or among close family members, irritations or resentment can cause a sense of isolation or lead to strained relationships, disrupting the peace that is vital for an environment of prayer and worship. Often, these feelings are amplified by the enemy as a tactic to hinder your spiritual focus and divert you from the purpose of your prayers. Recognizing these emotions and bringing them before God can help prevent their growth into bitterness, enabling you to stay aligned with His love and unity.

· Mind Wandering

One of the subtle yet common challenges during prayer is the tendency for the mind to drift away to unrelated thoughts and concerns. This distraction often occurs when your thoughts start to wander towards daily worries, tasks, or even random ideas, pulling you away from the prayer points at hand. Such mental drift can break the flow of spiritual engagement, creating a gap between you and the divine focus needed in prayer. The pull of these unrelated thoughts often comes from your surroundings or even inner anxieties, which can cloud your focus and reduce the power and effectiveness of your prayers. By becoming aware of these tendencies, you can actively combat mind-wandering through strategies such as grounding yourselves in the Word, taking a few moments to quiet your mind before starting, and gently redirecting your thoughts back to God each time you sense yourselves drifting.

· Slumber

As you begin to pray, you may suddenly feel a wave of tiredness washing over you; a seemingly inexplicable desire to sleep that can feel nearly impossible to shake off. This experience often signals a subtle form of spiritual opposition, a distraction intended to weaken your spirit, cloud your focus, and sap your resolve. Recognizing this feeling for what it is: an attempt to deter you from deepening your connection with God; empowers you to resist and press through with determination. Remember, God gives us strength when we are weak, and through prayer, we can call upon His power to overcome every form of distraction and spiritual resistance, including the temptation to succumb to slumber.

· Desire for Social Connection over Communion with God

In our daily lives, it's natural to feel a strong pull toward social interaction and connection with those around us. Human conversations, with their immediacy and familiarity, can often feel more rewarding or comforting in the moment than engaging in communion with God. This urge to connect socially can, at times, subtly overshadow your desire to focus on your spiritual relationship, drawing you into discussions that distract you from the deeper, more nourishing dialogue you're invited to have with God.

When you prioritize social connections above your communion with God, you may not realize how these interactions; though fulfilling on a surface level, can hinder your spiritual focus. It is in those moments of human distraction that you may miss opportunities to draw closer to God, to listen to His voice, and to receive the guidance, peace, and strength He offers to you. This challenge of choosing divine communion over human conversation requires a conscious shift, a reorientation of your hearts and minds, where you begin to place a higher value on moments of silence, prayer, and reflection.

In your quiet time, God speaks to you in ways that friends and family, no matter how well-meaning, cannot. Yet, it requires a disciplined heart to resist the tendency to seek immediate comfort in human interaction and instead lean into the rich, soul-deep communion that God offers.

· Difficulty in Vocalizing Prayer

At times, a heavy weight or inner reluctance can make it challenging to voice your prayers. This difficulty often arises especially when praying aloud or speaking in tongues. It may feel as though there is an unseen resistance, as if something is holding you back from freely expressing your heart and desires before God. This resistance can be subtle, manifesting as hesitancy, doubt, or even a fear of fully releasing your emotions and thoughts in His presence. In these moments, it's as though a barrier seeks to muffle your words, limit your boldness, and diminish your confidence in communicating with the Lord.

This heaviness may come from various factors; perhaps spiritual opposition, feelings of inadequacy, or even the enemy's attempt to hinder your connection with God. But it's crucial to remember that God delights in hearing from us, whether we speak in quiet whispers or loud declarations. Pushing through this resistance can lead to a breakthrough, bringing you to a place where prayer flows freely, unhindered by doubts or fears. Through perseverance and reliance on the Holy Spirit, you can find the strength to overcome this reluctance, allowing yourselves to be fully immersed in prayer and openly express yourselves before the Lord.

· Distractions like Social Media or Phone Notifications

In today's world, the allure of phones and social media has become a significant challenge for maintaining focus, particularly during prayer. The constant pings, alerts, and notifications can quickly shift your attention, even with the best intentions to concentrate on up-reach with God. Whether it's a message, a reminder, or a seemingly harmless notification, these interruptions can pull your minds away from the depth of prayer and disrupt the spiritual atmosphere you're trying to cultivate.

The subtlety of these distractions is that they often come masked as urgent, nudging you to check a message "just this once" or to respond to something that can likely wait. When you allow these interruptions to take precedence, however small, you invite fragmented attention, which hinders your ability to connect meaningfully with God. Genuine, undistracted prayer requires a set-aside time where God has your undivided attention. In this space, you commit not only to resist distractions but to revere the sacredness of this encounter, guarding it with intentionality and discipline.

One way to combat these distractions is to turn off notifications or place your phone on "Do Not Disturb" mode, allowing your spirit to be fully present without the world's interference.

· Discouraging Thoughts

As you enter deeper into prayer, especially when engaging in tongues or a spiritual language, you may encounter an inner voice sowing seeds of doubt and self-consciousness. This voice often questions the power and effectiveness of your prayers, subtly suggesting that your words may be inadequate, misunderstood, or without impact. These thoughts are attempts to undermine your faith, making you second-guess not only the worth of your prayers but also your connection to God Himself. These feelings can evoke a sense of insecurity or discomfort, especially when praying in ways that may feel beyond your full understanding. Yet it is vital to recognize that such thoughts are barriers, not truths. They seek to draw your focus away from the purpose of prayer and diminish your confidence in God's listening ear. When this happens, remember that these whispers of doubt are not reflections of reality but distractions to weaken the fervency of your intercession. Stand firm, knowing that every prayer offered in faith; whether in your natural language or the heavenly language of tongues, is both powerful and effective in the spiritual realm.

These and many other distractions serve as tools in the enemy's arsenal, specifically crafted to reduce your effectiveness in prayer. By identifying and standing against these tactics, you can reclaim your authority in prayer, focused on drawing near to God. Each of these distractions can be overcome by vigilance, determination, and reliance on the Holy Spirit.

As you grow in spiritual discernment, you can sidestep these interruptions, pressing on in faith and power, knowing that our prayers reach Heaven and that God is faithful to answer.

THE EVIL SPIRITS ALSO HINDER OTHER ASPECTS OF THE CHURCH.

Evil spirits relentlessly work to hinder various aspects of the Church's mission and purpose. They strive to prevent believers from spreading the gospel and introducing others to Christ. They oppose genuine Worship and attempt to stifle the hearts of worshipers, diverting focus from God. They discourage intercession: standing in the gap for others, for the Church, for cities, and even for nations. They resist acts of charity and mission work, casting doubt or creating obstacles to prevent the love of God from reaching those in need. They seek to disrupt your study of the Scriptures, attempting to distract or discourage believers from digging deeper into God's Word and growing in understanding.

Their mission is crystal clear: to thwart and destroy the abundant life that Christ came to give us. As Jesus said in *John 10:10*, *"The thief comes only to steal, kill, and destroy; I have come that they may have life, and have it to the full."* The enemy's agenda is destruction; he wants to extinguish the light of faith, erode believers' joy, and derail their purpose.

But how does the enemy do this? *Matthew 13: 24-25* provides a vivid picture: *"Another parable put He forth unto them, saying, The Kingdom of Heaven is likened unto a man who sowed good seed in his field. But while men slept, his enemy came and sowed tares among the wheat, and went his way."*

This parable warns us about the dangers of spiritual sleep and complacency. When you are not spiritually vigilant; when you are inattentive or indifferent, the enemy gains access to sow seeds of discord, doubt, and deception in your lives and within the Church. He uses these seeds to hinder your growth, disturb unity, and cause confusion.

To counteract these tactics, you must remain spiritually awake, alert, and diligent in prayer. Prayer is your greatest defence against the attacks of the enemy. It is crucial to pray day and night, engaging in constant communion with God to strengthen yourselves and intercede for others. 1 Thessalonians 5:17 encourages us to *"pray continually,"* a reminder that consistent, focused, and fervent prayer is essential for successful spiritual warfare.

Effective prayer requires perseverance and dedication. At times, this may mean spending extended hours in prayer; one, two, three, or even more hours daily, to see breakthroughs and victories in your spiritual lives and ministries. Through sustained prayer, you invite God's power to work mightily, overcoming the enemy's schemes and advancing God's Kingdom here on Earth. Let us, therefore, not grow weary but commit to a lifestyle of devoted, powerful, and unceasing prayer, trusting that God will guard and guide us in every endeavour.

How to Pray for a Longer Time?

When I first gave my life to the Lord, I often wondered, *How can I pray for a longer time?* I could only manage a few minutes at a time up to an hour a day. But now, after more than 30 years in ministry, I can confidently say that prayer is something we learn, practice, and grow in daily as we dedicate ourselves to it. Spending time with God becomes the most precious part of life, because you come to know Jesus as your Master, Lord, Friend, and All in All. You'll find joy in sharing everything with Him; *that* is the essence of prayer.

As your prayer life deepens, so will your confidence in speaking to the Father. At some point, the Holy Spirit will raise a standard within you against the enemy; you'll find yourself binding and loosing, uprooting and planting, all in the Name of Jesus Christ. This is what prayer is truly about; the creative power of prayer at work through God. As it is written in Jeremiah 1:10: *"See, I have this day set thee over the nations and over the kingdoms, to root out, and to pull down, and to destroy, and to throw down, to build, and to plant."*

To cultivate longer, focused prayer times, begin by creating a quiet, undistracted atmosphere. Set the tone with worship; whether by singing or playing confessional worship songs. Stay centred; you can close your eyes, lift your hands, kneel, stand, or move as you feel led. Just keep alert and present in His presence.

WHAT HAPPENS WHEN YOU DO NOT PRAY?

Isaiah 40:31 gives a powerful assurance: *"But they that wait upon the Lord shall renew their strength;* (prayerlessness makes you weaker spiritually) *they shall mount up with wings as eagles;* (they will rise above the storms and soar in the heights God has prepared for them, like an eagle soaring, not stumbling like a chicken) *they shall run, and not be weary;* (with a life anchored in prayer, you can run the race of faith without growing weary) and *they shall walk, and not faint."* This passage underscores the strength, resilience, and empowerment that come from a consistent, dedicated prayer life.

Prayerlessness, on the other hand, is spiritually dangerous. When we neglect prayer, we become vulnerable to discouragement, temptation, and defeat. Often, prayerlessness is rooted in a life burdened by sin. We see this in the story of Adam and Eve in the Garden of Eden. After disobeying God, they became afraid and hid from The Father. Genesis 3: 8-9 illustrates this moment of separation: *"They heard the sound of the Lord God walking in the garden in the cool of the day, and the man and his wife hid themselves from the presence of the Lord God among the trees of the garden. Then the Lord God called to the man, and said to him, 'Where are you?'"* The sin in their hearts created a divide, pulling them away from the presence of the One who could restore and forgive.

But through Christ, we have a path to forgiveness, cleansing, and restoration. When we bring our sins to Him in sincere repentance, He not only forgives us but also empowers us to overcome and have dominion over sin. No longer do we need to hide from God; instead, we can seek refuge in Him. We need to run to God, not from Him, trusting that He is always ready to embrace and strengthen us when we turn to Him.

I pray earnestly that your prayer life becomes stronger, deeply rooted, and mighty. In prayer, we access the fullness of God's promises, His strength, and His guidance. A life empowered by prayer allows you to walk with resilience, soar to new spiritual heights, and experience the fulfilment of God's promises.

1. When you neglect prayer, your emotions begin to dominate your decisions, and the works of the flesh gain greater influence over your life. Without the discipline and guidance that prayer provides, you become more susceptible to agitation and restlessness. A lack of prayer diminishes your confidence and spiritual stability, leading you to make decisions impulsively and based solely on fleeting emotions rather than divine wisdom.

Anger becomes harder to control, often resulting in harsh words or actions that you later regret. You may find yourself drawing unnecessary boundaries, engaging in conflicts without just cause, or even battling feelings of bitterness and resentment. In such a state, your speech becomes excessive and careless, often leading to misunderstandings or strife.

Furthermore, when prayer is absent, discernment diminishes, and you become more prone to seeking comfort or validation in the wrong places. This could mean associating with the wrong friends or environments that pull you further away from God's plan for your life. You may begin to entertain unhealthy habits, compromise on your values, and stray from the path of righteousness.

Without the protective power of prayer, it is easy to fall into these traps. Prayer anchors your heart, mind, and spirit in God's truth. It keeps you aligned with His will, fortifies you against the temptations of the flesh, and renews your strength to live a life that glorifies God. Remember, a prayerless life is a powerless life; guard your prayer time diligently to stay rooted in God's grace and wisdom.

2. When prayer ceases, the lifeline of communion with God weakens.

Demonic powers understand that a life without prayer is a life without spiritual defence. When prayer ceases, the lifeline of communion with God weakens, and the believer's fellowship with Him becomes constricted or, in some cases, almost non-existent. In the absence of prayer, you risk falling under the influence and control of these dark powers, whose primary goal is to disrupt your relationship with God and hinder you from fulfilling His purpose.

When someone is placed under the realm of demonic influence, they are susceptible to a host of traps that draw them further from God. These forces employ various methods to ensnare souls, using sin as their primary weapon. This sin can manifest in many forms; idolatry, hatred, violence, addictions, anger, depression, despair, immorality, theft, sexual sins, blasphemy, gluttony, witchcraft, drunkenness, and a rebellious heart that disregards God's commandments. Lies and deceit cloud the mind, while shame and guilt build layers of bondage, obscuring the path back to God. Every manifestation of sin is a strategy to gain control and keep people enslaved to darkness.

When demonic forces dominate, the works of the flesh rise and overshadow the spirit, which has been weakened by prayerlessness. The absence of spiritual resilience through prayer makes it challenging to resist the pull of these temptations, which continue to lead people further away from the life of freedom that God intended. Left unchecked, these forces can drag a person into a downward spiral, damaging their soul, body, and relationships.

This is why Jesus Christ our Lord Himself warned of the importance of spiritual readiness, teaching that, to overcome these forces, we must first *"bind the strong man"* before reclaiming what he has taken (Matthew 12:29). This binding is accomplished through persistent, fervent prayer. Prayer is our means of waging war against these spiritual enemies, breaking their power, and reclaiming our place in God's presence. Through prayer, we gain the authority to sever these chains and walk in the liberty and peace that come from God's Spirit.

3. When you do not pray you can easily backslide and lose your trust in God.

When you do not pray, you risk losing your anointing entirely. This sobering reality is evident in the lives of biblical figures like Saul, Judas, and others who drifted away from God. Prayer sustains the anointing; it is the spiritual lifeline that connects us to God's presence and power. Without it, the heart becomes vulnerable to sin, pride, and distraction.

Consider Saul, the first king of Israel. Chosen and anointed by God, he started his journey with promise and potential. Yet, as he distanced himself from God's presence and neglected obedience, his anointing was stripped away. The tragic words of 2 Samuel 1: 21 echo the gravity of his downfall:

"Ye mountains of Gilboa, let there be no dew, neither let there be rain, upon you, nor fields of offerings: for there the shield of the mighty is vilely cast away, the shield of Saul, as though he had not been anointed with oil."

The shield of Saul, once a symbol of divine favour and strength, was discarded; a painful reminder that the anointing is not permanent without prayer and dependence on God.

Likewise, Judas Iscariot, who walked with Jesus and witnessed countless miracles, forfeited his place among the apostles. His betrayal was not an overnight decision but the result of a heart that became disconnected from the sustaining power of God's presence. Without prayer, his soul became susceptible to deception, greed, and ultimately despair.

When a believer ceases to pray, they risk falling into spiritual stagnation and eventual separation from God. Jesus' words in Matthew 7:23 warn of this stark reality: *"And then I will declare to them, 'I never knew you; depart from Me, you who practice lawlessness.'"* This is not merely a loss of spiritual gifts or abilities but a loss of intimacy with the very Source of life and purpose.

The absence of prayer leads to a spiritual drought, just as the mountains of Gilboa. Without the refreshing dew of God's Spirit, the soul becomes dry, the work of ministry becomes mechanical, and the once-anointed life begins to unravel.

Prayer is not optional for those who carry the anointing; it is a necessity. It anchors us in God's will, protects us from falling into sin, and renews the oil of the Spirit upon our lives. To neglect prayer is to neglect the anointing, and to neglect the anointing is to risk becoming spiritually ineffective. Let the lives of Saul and Judas serve as solemn reminders of the cost of abandoning prayer.

In contrast, let us remain steadfast in prayer, seeking God's face daily, that His presence may rest upon us and His anointing flow continually, empowering us to fulfill His purpose.

4. When you do not pray your faith is diminished; fear enters, you begin to fear even the very things you used to resist easily before. Fear is the direct opposite of faith, you begin to question the Power of God, some go into panics, attacks and torments.

5. When you neglect to pray, you create an opening for the enemy to gain strength and influence over your life. Prayer is a powerful spiritual weapon designed by God to shield us from the enemy's attacks and to keep us grounded in His truth. When you choose not to pray, you forfeit the divine protection and empowerment that prayer provides. Without regular communication with God through prayer, your spiritual defences become weakened, and one becomes more susceptible to the subtle and often deceptive tactics of the enemy. In this weakened state, the enemy can slowly creep in, gradually eroding the faith, peace, and joy. Over time, this lack of prayer can lead to spiritual complacency, and if one is not careful, he may find himself once again entangled in the very bonds Christ has already set him free from.

It is through consistent and fervent prayer that we keep ourselves aligned with God's will and maintain the strength to resist the enemy's schemes. Prayer is not only a way to ask for what we need, but it is a means of surrendering our hearts and lives to God's control, allowing Him to strengthen and protect us. Without prayer, one is vulnerable to spiritual attack, and the enemy can bring people back into bondage, ensnaring them in old habits, fears, or destructive patterns. Prayer enables us to stay vigilant, to stand firm in the freedom Christ has won for us, and to actively resist the lies and temptations of the enemy.

The more one neglects prayer, the greater the foothold the enemy gains, and the harder it becomes to break free from his grasp. Prayer is not just an occasional practice; it is essential to our spiritual survival and growth, keeping us free and empowered to walk in the victory that Jesus has already secured for us.

6. When you do not pray the Land can become defiled, corrupt, immoral and unethical.

2 Chronicles 7:14 *"If my people, which are called by My name, shall humble themselves, and pray, and seek My face, and turn from their wicked ways; then will I hear from heaven, and will forgive their sin, and will heal their land."*

7. When you fail to engage in prayer, you put your very protection in jeopardy. The shield of God's presence that should surround you begins to diminish, leaving you exposed to the forces of darkness and the harsh realities of life. Without the covering of prayer, your heart may feel vulnerable, and you may start to experience a sense of disconnection from God. It's as if you are navigating a world of chaos with no sense of direction, no one to guide you, and no refuge in sight. In such times, it can seem as though God is distant, leaving you feeling abandoned, forsaken, and lonely; like no one truly cares about your struggles or your needs. The weight of the world may press heavily upon you, and you may begin to wonder if anyone notices, let alone if anyone is willing to stand by your side.

But the moment you begin to pray, the situation begins to shift. Prayer is not merely an act of communication; it is a powerful invitation for God to intervene in your life.

When you turn your heart toward God, you open the door to His protection and provision. Prayer allows you to draw near to God, and in doing so, His presence begins to fill your life once again, restoring your peace and safety. You are reminded that you are not alone, that you are seen, known, and loved by a caring

Father who is always present, even when it feels like the world is falling apart. It is in the sacred space of prayer that you begin to understand the depths of God's care for you, and He reassures you that He is watching over you, shielding you from harm and guiding you with His wisdom.

Moreover, prayer is a means by which God opens your life to divine relationships. As you connect with God through prayer, He may send people into your life who genuinely care for you; people who will encourage you, support you, and stand by you through the ups and downs. These are not mere coincidences, but divine appointments. God uses prayer as a way to orchestrate connections that will help you grow, heal, and flourish. He knows exactly what you need, and in His perfect timing, He will provide the people who will walk alongside you and bear your burdens.

When you pray, you are not only speaking to God; you are also allowing Him to work in you and through you. Prayer nourishes your soul, providing spiritual sustenance that strengthens you in times of weakness. It enables you to rise above the challenges of life and face them with renewed strength, knowing that you are covered and upheld by God's grace. Prayer opens the door for God to send not only spiritual strength but also physical and emotional support through the people He places in your life. Those who truly care, who are sent by God to walk with you, will become a tangible manifestation of His love and faithfulness.

Ultimately, prayer is a constant reminder that you are never alone. It is a privilege to have access to the Creator of the universe, and through prayer, you experience the profound truth that God is always with you. He knows your every need, and through prayer, He brings His sustaining power into your life. As you continue to pray, you will find not only protection and sustenance but also the deep assurance that God's care is always available to you.

8. When you neglect to pray regularly, the consequences on your spiritual life are profound and far-reaching. Prayer is not just an activity, but the essential lifeline that keeps you connected to God, and without it, your ability to discern His voice and recognize His guidance weakens. As the distance between you and God grows, your spiritual sensitivity becomes dull, and you begin to lose clarity of vision. The power of discernment, which is vital for navigating life's challenges, becomes diminished. You struggle to distinguish between God's will and your own desires, and what once seemed clear in the light of God's truth becomes clouded by confusion.

Moreover, a lack of consistent prayer causes your faith to gradually erode. Faith is not something that can remain stagnant; it either grows stronger through constant communion with God, or it weakens when neglected. When you do not pray enough, your hearts and minds become vulnerable to doubt, and your confidence in God's promises begins to falter. As this doubt takes hold, you find it increasingly difficult to believe even the most basic truths of your faith. Things that you once trusted with unwavering certainty begin to feel distant, hard to grasp, or even unreachable. This is because doubt has crept in, and it takes root in your hearts, pushing out the firm belief that once kept you anchored in God's truth.

When prayer is neglected, you unknowingly open the door for the enemy to sow seeds of fear, confusion, and unbelief into your hearts. These seeds grow into destructive thoughts and attitudes that further hinder your ability to walk in faith. The more you drift from prayer, the harder it becomes to remember the power of God that once seemed so evident in your lives. Somebody starts to struggle with feelings of isolation, questioning God's presence and His willingness to act on his behalf. What was once so clear: your identity in Christ, His promises of provision, protection, and guidance, becomes clouded by the storm of doubt.

Prayer is not just a religious duty; it is the means through which you sustain your spiritual life and protect your hearts from the attacks of the enemy. It is the source of your strength, your peace, and your victory. Without it, one is like a tree cut off from its roots, unable to draw the nourishment needed to survive. The more you pray, the more your faith is built up, and the clearer you can see God's purposes for your lives.

Prayer keeps you grounded in truth, reminding you of who you are in Christ, and empowering you to stand firm in the face of adversity.

9. When you do not pray you can no more see clearly spiritually; you can hardly remember your dreams and visions; your communication channel with God becomes crowdy. If you are a prophet, instead of "Thus says The Lord..." your language becomes, "I do not know very well but I think I saw, I think I heard..." That is very dangerous.

Draw near to God, and He will draw near to you. This beautiful promise invites us into a deeper relationship with our Creator, one built on prayer, worship, and attentive listening. Prayer is not just a ritual; it is the key to unlocking the presence of God in your lives. When you make it a daily habit, setting aside time to communicate with God, you are inviting His power, peace, and guidance into your hearts.

In the stillness of prayer, you come before God with worship, adoration, and gratitude, acknowledging His majesty and the greatness of His love. But prayer is not one-sided. It is also a time to listen to God's voice: attuning your hearts to His whispers, receiving His wisdom, and aligning your will with His purpose for your lives. As you draw near to God, you experience His nearness in a profound and transformative way.

Let prayer be the heartbeat of your day, and in that sacred space, allow your soul to connect with God. Worship Him in spirit and truth, and open your heart to His voice. For as we draw near to God, He promises that He will draw near to us, guiding us, comforting us, and empowering us to walk in His will. Amen

We must remain steadfast in prayer, continuing to seek God's will with persistence and faith until we see the desired results manifest according to His divine purpose.

Prayer is not a one-time event, but a continuous journey of alignment with God's heart, where we learn to wait on His timing and trust in His sovereignty. We must press forward in prayer, understanding that God's plans for us are good, and He will answer in His perfect way and timing. It is through unwavering commitment in prayer that we can see God's will unfold in our lives, knowing that He hears every voice and responds in ways that are best for us. Let us not grow weary but persist in fervent prayer, knowing that God rewards those who diligently seek Him.

CHAPTER 3

PRAYER IS
CREATIVE BY GOD

CHAPTER 3

PRAYER IS CREATIVE BY GOD

GOD CREATED ALL THINGS BY THE POWER OF HIS WORD

If we want to have the nature of God, if we need to be in His image, after His likeness and according to His resemblance as God intended for us at creation, then we need to try to do the things that God is teaching us to do. Speaking things in prayer in His Name and believing that they can be materialized by faith in God.

Hebrews 11: 3 « Through faith we understand that *the worlds were framed by the Word of GOD, so that things which are seen were not made of things which do appear.* »

With prayer we can be creative by God, but that does not make us to become gods. Obviously Adam and Eve misunderstood this theory of God when they were under satan's inspiration that is why they ate the fruit of the tree of the knowledge of good and evil. The truth is, at first they knew no evil, they knew only the good part of everything, and God intended to keep it that way, to make things easier for them.

Adam gave the names of all the animals and it was acceptable to God.

Yet the one who sabotaged their pleasure with God was well aware that after they have eaten of the fruit, they will be confronted with the challenging effect of choices. The choice between good and evil;

See, the devil had already chosen evil, he needed some company with him. Exactly the same way he does with humans continually today, so that he will be telling himself: by the way he is not the only one in that situation but also the beloved of God: humans. That is why we are presented the choice with a clear hint of choosing life so that we and our descendants may live with God for Eternity.

We need to speak good and positive things over our lives, over our children, over our family: blessings, supply, prosperity, abundance of life, growth, multiplication, happiness, wisdom, peace, good health, long life, joy and more in JESUS CHRIST's name.

I often say to my brethren, to my family and to anyone around me: God bless you! One day my son told my husband: Papa, Mama blesses you so much that I think you have a life full of blessings; my husband said that is true son, and I said listen baby I am believing that by my blessings God will overrule all the evil words that might have been pronounced over him in the past, so that those possible evil pronouncements might vanish by the multitude of my blessings; that is what gives us a blessed family in our God.

Perhaps you might have been cursed by somebody while you were growing up or some time in your life by someone you know or not. But if you take the habit of reversing the curses in prayer and pronouncing blessings over yourself every day, sooner you will be so blessed physically and spiritually that you will become a blessing to many in the Name of The Lord Jesus.

THE ESSENTIALITY OF AGREEMENT

The prayers we offer in Church don't need to be like a routine, but meaningful and creative over the Church. The Lord Jesus-Christ said in

Matthew 21: 13 *"My House shall be called the House of prayer".*

The primary reason to gather in Church should be to pray and ask for more power and anointing to go into the world and live successfully as Christians. We need to teach people more, and practice more the act of fellowshipping and communing with God in prayer in Church for the Church.

Great praise and worship time in Church is amazing, but other things like games, open dance show should not take the place of prayer in church. It is true that because some people also are not inclined to pray, the battle over prayer becomes challenging. When we say let us pray, you will see some people looking so tired and even angry. Prayer should not be annoying, it is a great privilege to commune with Our Creator; The Almighty God Who Alone can give us life, wisdom, and all blessings without sorrow to His Glory.

In *The Creative Power of Prayer*, the Lord's words, *"Watch and pray, that you enter not into temptation"*, serve as a profound reminder of the importance of staying spiritually vigilant (Matthew 26: 41). May we, as the body of Christ, grow in our love for agreement prayers in the Church, lifting our voices together in unity to call upon the Lord for a spiritual revival. The world is in desperate need of this awakening, and it begins with fervent, collective prayer.

Let us commit to praying more, with hearts full of faith and expectancy. As James 4: 2 reminds us, *"You have not because you ask not."* It is through prayer that we access God's power to transform lives, bring healing, and spark the revival we long to see in our communities and beyond.

The Ministry is a spiritual Endeavour; it cannot be advanced by the armour of the flesh, only the principles of The Lord Jesus can work when it comes to advancing the Church of Christ on earth.

The book of Mark really shows us the result of the prayers that the Lord Jesus-Christ made on earth. He was quick and prompt in helping people because He was always filled with the Power of God through prayer.

I have come to understand the profound significance of a disciplined prayer life. The most powerful example we have is our Lord Jesus Christ, who demonstrated a life rooted in daily communion with the Father. Mark 1: 35 tells us that *"Jesus rose early in the morning, long before daylight, and went to a solitary place to pray"*. This is not a casual practice but a vital part of ministry and relationship with God.

When we gather in the house of the Lord, we enter a sacred space where the burdens of life can be laid down before a loving Father. It is a place where prayers ascend like sweet incense, and divine answers descend to transform our circumstances. The Church is not just a physical building but a spiritual meeting point; a place where Heaven touches Earth, and where we, as God's people, find peace, strength, and solutions for every care we bring before Him.

If Jesus, the Son of God, felt the need to pray so often, how much more should we, as His followers, embrace prayer as an essential part of our lives? His example shows us that prayer is not merely a duty but a lifeline.

He was God in the flesh, the perfect union of divinity and humanity, fully embodying the presence and power of God. In contrast, people are born as mere flesh, limited and disconnected from the fullness of spiritual life until they encounter God. When you come to believe in Him, surrendering your heart and life, a miraculous transformation begins. Through faith, your spirit; once dormant, is quickened and made alive by the indwelling Holy Spirit. It is through prayer, the divine channel of communication with God becomes vibrant and active. Prayer breathes life into your spirit, aligning you with God's will, empowering you to walk in His purpose, and enabling you to experience His presence in a deeply personal way.

Prayer is a privilege, it gives you a strong conviction in God. If you do not have conviction as a Christian you will just be falling and rising. I pray you will not fall in the Name of Our Lord Jesus-Christ.

Christianity is not speculative, it is not hypothetical: like "I will try it, perhaps it will work". Christianity is a conviction. God means all that He is asking us to do, for our own good.

The more we pray, the more we align our lives according to the Mind and the plan of God.

We (The Church) are the only hope to the world. They do not see Our God but they see us.

They try to look for the difference in us as Christians and if they realize that we are just a group of complainers, worried and anxious people who rely on no hope, how will they bother to follow Our God? When we pray, we don't complain.

David said in Psalms 79: 9-10

"Help us, O God of our salvation, for the glory of Thy name: and deliver us, and purge away our sins, for Thy name's sake. Wherefore should the heathen say, Where is their God?"

Luke 6: 12-13 *"And it came to pass in those days, that He went out into a mountain to pray, and continued all night in prayer to God. And when it was day, He called unto Him his disciples: and of them He chose twelve, whom also He named apostles;"*

Through prayer God leads us into making major decisions, like here we see that the Lord Jesus-Christ prayed consistently for a whole night before choosing His disciples. In the ministry and even in our families in every situation, it is important and vital to pray and hear from God before taking the step to make decisions.

Luke 9: 18, *"And it came to pass, as He was alone praying, his disciples were with Him: and He asked them, saying, Whom say the people that I am ?"*

Luke 9: 28-29 *"And it came to pass about an eight days after these sayings, He took Peter and John and James, and went up into a mountain to pray. And as He prayed, the fashion of His countenance was altered, and His raiment was white and glistering."*

The Lord Jesus-Christ prayed *always* at every moment of the day and everywhere. Before the Transfiguration The Lord prayed.

Our Lord prayed so often and so pertinently that at a point the disciples asked Him to teach them to pray.

Luke 11: 1 *"And it came to pass, that, as He was praying in a certain place, when He ceased, one of his disciples said unto Him, Lord, teach us to pray, as John also taught his disciples."*

As someone may hear you pray, would they also say to you 'please teach us to pray' ? The Lord just told them listen when you pray say: (The Lord's Prayer) and that is the teaching we shall speak about in the last chapter of this book.

A brother once said, *"I don't know how to pray, and I don't hear the voice of God."*

It's understandable to feel this way, but the good news is that prayer can be learned. You might ask, *"How?"* Begin by studying the prayers recorded in the Bible. Invite the Holy Spirit to guide and teach you. Remember, prayer requires learning and practice.

Don't be misled by the notion that the ability to pray will simply descend upon you without effort. The truth is, effective prayer aligns with the Word of God, which reflects His will. To pray in a way that pleases God, you must study the Scriptures and observe how others prayed; Jesus Christ, the apostles, and faithful servants of God like Abraham, David, Daniel, Esther, Anna, and many more.

Without this foundation, you might be praying, but not in the most effective way. Learning from the Bible equips you to communicate with God in a way that is both meaningful and powerful.

It is the Holy Spirit who breathes life and power into our prayers, ensuring they align with God's will and reach His throne effectively. Consider this: if you were to meet a king or the president of a nation, you would need to learn the appropriate protocol: how to speak, when to bow, and even table manners. You wouldn't approach them casually, or using inappropriate language. Such actions would be out of place and unacceptable.

So, when we approach God in prayer, we must do so with reverence and respect. Our words should honour His majesty, and our posture whether bowing, standing with lifted hands, sitting in humility, or prostrating before Him should reflect our deep awe and submission.

Prayer is an act of worship, a time to commune with our Creator meaningfully and sincerely.

This reverent approach can be learned and cultivated. By praying regularly, we become familiar with conversing with our

Heavenly Father in a manner that is honourable, respectful, and simple. Through practice and the leading of the Holy Spirit, we grow in our ability to approach Him with the dignity and reverence He deserves.

John 17: Jesus' Prayer for Us; The Church

The book of John chapter 17 reveals how our Lord Jesus prayed for us, and for the Church. This prayer demonstrates His deep love and intercession, showing us the example of standing in the gap for others.

PERSISTENT PRAYER: THE KEY TO BREAKTHROUGH

In Luke 18:1, Jesus taught:

"And He spake a parable unto them to this end, that men ought always to pray, and not to faint."

One vital lesson in prayer is the importance of persistence. Praying until we see results. For instance, I prayed for ten years for my children. During that season, I also prayed for other young women desiring children, and I witnessed God answer their prayers. I would even carry their babies during consecrations at church. Despite waiting for my own miracle, I kept loving and celebrating children because my faith assured me that God's promise would come to pass.

God gave me a specific Rhema word:

"I will love you, I will bless you, I will multiply you, and I will bless the fruit of your womb."

I held onto this promise, praying earnestly toward its fulfilment. True to His word, God was faithful and fulfilled what He had promised.

The Bible contains many promises of God, but they require our active faith in prayer for their manifestation. As Hebrews 11:1 reminds us:

"Now faith is the substance of things hoped for, the evidence of things not seen."

The Drive Behind Prayer: The Love for God

One of the greatest motivators for a consistent prayer life is our love for God. When we truly love Him with all our heart, soul, mind, and strength, prayer becomes a joyful act of communion rather than a duty. We are drawn to His presence, where we feel safe and deeply fulfilled.

God desires our love to be unconditional. Not just for what He can do for us, but for Who He is and what He has already done. He loved us unconditionally first, even while we were sinners, undeserving of His grace. Because of His great love, He saved us and called us into ministry with Him.

Be Persistent and Obedient

God's promises require us to persist in prayer and obey Him without hesitation. As we walk in faith and align our lives with His word, He is faithful to fulfill every promise.

THE PRAYER OF JABEZ

1 Chronicles 4:10

"And Jabez called on the God of Israel, saying,
Oh that thou wouldest bless me indeed,
and enlarge my coast,
and that thine hand might be with me,
and that thou wouldest keep me from evil,
that it may not grieve me!
And God granted him that which he requested."

Jabez prayed fervently for God's blessings, asking Him to remove all curses from his life and transform him into a source of blessing. He sought the divine exchange of sorrow for joy, pleading for the garment of blessings to replace the garment of sorrow.

Furthermore, Jabez prayed for God to enlarge his territory. Acknowledging the limitations of his current portion, he boldly requested an expansion of his boundaries: a larger plot of land and increased property; aspiring to become a landowner in his time.

The most profound aspect of Jabez's prayer, however, was his plea for the Hand of the Lord to be with him. This request reflected a deep understanding of God's power and presence. As David declared in Psalm 89:13, *"You have a strong arm; Your hand is mighty, Your right hand is exalted."* Jabez recognized that with God's mighty Hand guiding and empowering him, every other request would be fulfilled in divine alignment.

The Hand of the Lord Can:

- Anoint you
- Bless you
- Buckle you (strengthen and prepare you)
- Comfort you
- Correct you
- Carry you
- Cover you
- Defend you
- Deliver you
- Elevate you
- Embrace you
- Feed you
- Fight for you
- Guide you
- Help you
- Hold you
- Instruct you
- Keep you
- Lead you
- Prosper you
- Protect you
- Reward you
- Save you
- Shield you

- Sustain you
- Uphold you

The Hand of the Lord can do all things.

Glory to God!

Jabez prayed, saying, *"Oh, that You would keep me from evil!"* This is indeed a powerful prayer, asking God to protect him from all evil, for He alone has the power to do so.

Jabez also prayed against anger, recognizing it as a strategy of the enemy to distract and accuse God's children. And the Lord, who is faithful to answer prayers, granted all that Jabez requested.

Hallelujah! That is the Lord our God.

The One who answers prayers!

CREATIVE CONFESSIONS TO DECLARE OVER YOUR LIFE IN PRAYER

I am a dwelling place of the Holy Spirit of God.

I am built up together with other children of God into a Holy Habitation for His presence. The Word of God declares that I am a royal priesthood, a holy nation, a chosen generation, and a peculiar person set apart to reveal His glory to the nations.

I am special in the sight of God.

Because I believe in and receive Jesus Christ, I have been given the power to become a child of God. I am empowered to trample on serpents and scorpions and overcome all the power of the enemy.

I walk in the authority of Jesus Christ.

I am empowered to use the Name of Jesus to cast out demons, heal the sick, bind and loose according to His Word. Whatever I bind on earth is bound in heaven, and whatever I loose on earth is loosed in heaven.

I carry the keys of the Kingdom.

The keys of the Kingdom of Heaven are entrusted to me. As a member of the Body of Christ: The Church; the gates of hell cannot prevail against me.

I am a branch in the true Vine.

Jesus Christ is the true Vine, and because I abide in Him, I bear the fruit of the Spirit in abundance: love, joy, peace, patience, kindness, goodness, faithfulness, gentleness, and self-control.

I am full of divine favour and blessings.

The grace of God shines upon my life like the light of His glory. I am a partaker of all the spiritual blessings of heaven, and His favour surrounds me like a shield.

I am an Overcomer.

The Bible declares, *"For whatsoever is born of God overcometh the world: and this is the victory that overcometh the world, even our faith"*

(1 John 5: 4). Therefore, in faith, I overcome ungodly worry, anxiety, heaviness of spirit, sorrow, depression, and the lust of the eyes and flesh, in Jesus' name.

Victory Over the Enemy

By faith, I have triumphed over all the devices of the enemy, for it is written, *"Greater is He that is in me than he that is in the world"* (1 John 4: 4). I am victorious in Jesus' name.

Multiplying Joy and Favour

My joy multiplies today and every day as I walk in unlimited favour through the name of Jesus.

Strength Through Christ

Nothing is impossible for me because I am in Christ. As it is written in Philippians 4: 13, *"I can do all things through Christ which strengtheneth me."*

Spirit of Favour

Oh Lord, let Your Spirit of favour lead me to unlimited success and blessings throughout this month and all the days of my life, in the name of Jesus.

Favour That Reigns in my life

Let God's favour reign in my life today and forever. I declare that I am a victorious child of God.

Right Timing and Opportunities

Lord, guide me to be at the right place at the right time, in Jesus' name.

Dismantling Opposition

I dismantle every opposition fighting against me, in Jesus' mighty name.

Reversal of Rejection

Those who once rejected me will now open doors for me, in the name of Jesus.

Receiving Total Favour

I receive total favour and victory in every area of my life, in Jesus' name.

Blessings That Follow

Wherever I go, let Your blessings follow me, in Jesus' name.

Guidance of the Holy Spirit

Holy Spirit, direct me into the wonderful things You have prepared for me, in Jesus' name. As it is written in John 16: 13, "*When He, the Spirit of Truth, is come, He will guide you into all truth: for He shall not speak of Himself; but whatsoever He shall hear, that shall He speak: and He will shew you things to come.*"

I am the head and not the tail; I will succeed and not fail because Christ dwells richly in me.

The Lord shall make me the head and not the tail; I will always be above and never beneath, as I hearken to the commandments of the Lord my God, observing and doing them. (*Deuteronomy 28: 13*).

God, arise and bless the works of my hands so that Your name may be glorified.

Deuteronomy 28: 12 *"The LORD shall open unto thee (me) His good treasure, the heaven to give the rain unto thy land in his season, and to bless all the work of thine hand: and thou shalt lend unto many nations, and thou shalt not borrow."*

Lord, help me to meditate on Your Word day and night so that I may prosper in all things.

Psalm 1: 2-3 *"But his (my) delight is in the law of the LORD; and in his law doth he meditate day and night. And he shall be like a tree planted by the rivers of water, that bringeth forth his fruit in his season; his leaf also shall not wither; and whatsoever he doeth shall prosper."*

I receive clarity on the wonderful opportunities at my disposal in the name of Jesus.

Lord, bless me so that I may bless others and be a blessing in my environment in Jesus' name.

Lord, I declare that I am blessed to be a blessing to the poor, orphans, and widows in the name of Jesus. Pure religion before God is to visit the fatherless and widows in their affliction and to remain unspotted from the world. (James 1: 27)

I declare that my eyes are open to recognize all the potentials You have blessed me with, and I use them to be a blessing in the name of Jesus.

I will not take for granted the blessings and favour You have poured into my life in the name of Jesus.

Oh Lord, I declare that I am delivered from a mind of procrastination and laziness in the name of Jesus.

Oh Lord, I am clothed with the garment of favour, enabling me to expand Your Kingdom wherever I go in the name of Jesus.

Father, I declare that I am empowered to be obedient to Your Word so that my life is prosperous. Your Word will not depart from my mouth; I will meditate on it day and night, and I will observe to do all that is written in it. For then, I will make my way prosperous and have good success. (Joshua 1: 8)

Every doubt that has become a stronghold in my life is broken down in the name of Jesus.

I banish anxiety and stress from my life and destroy their hold over me in the name of Jesus.

I reject every attitude of timidity and declare a mind of boldness in the name of Jesus.

Any relationships that would sabotage my destiny are broken in the name of Jesus.

Lord, I receive a spirit of excellence, enabling me to rise in my calling and glorify Your name. Like Daniel, I declare that an excellent spirit resides in me. (Daniel 6: 3)

Thank You, Lord, for answering my prayers.

Heavenly Father, I fully commit my plans and programs into Your hands, and I trust You to help me establish them. (Proverbs 16: 3)

Lord, let Your peace, which surpasses all understanding, saturate my mind, body, and soul in the name of Jesus. (Philippians 4: 7)

God Almighty, I declare that success manifests in every area of my life so that Your name is glorified.

Lord God, I trust You to show me favour wherever I go and wherever I turn in the name of Jesus.

I declare with assurance that I am victorious in the name of Jesus. Your thoughts toward me are thoughts of peace and not of evil, to give me an expected end. (Jeremiah 29: 11)

My God is able to do beyond what I think, ask, or imagine. Unto Him who is able to do exceeding abundantly above all that I ask or think, according to the power that works in me, I give all the glory. (Ephesians 3: 20) Amen!

You can also make these confessions over your spouse, your children and loved ones and over the Church. Amen!

THE TABERNACLE FORMULA

The tabernacle formula of prayer will allow you to pray non-stop for as long as three to four hours at a go. Following the tabernacle stages in prayer and visualizing the Lord at work by the power of the Holy Spirit, you can pray for as long as you desire.

The Tabernacle was the dwelling place of God where He met His people when they travelled through the desert in the time of Moses. As they entered the Tabernacle they passed through seven stations as a protocol to God's presence. Today, these same steps can help us connect with God and lead us through important elements of prayer.

1. The Outer Court; The Place of Thanksgiving and Praise

"Enter his gates with thanksgiving and his courts with praise; give thanks to him and praise his name." Psalm 100:4. As the people of God entered the Tabernacle, they came in with thanksgiving on their lips. Thanking God for all the blessings in your life is a great way to begin.

Every day, think of a fresh reason why you love and appreciate God.

2. The Brazen Altar - The Cross of Jesus

Praise the LORD, my soul, and forget not all his benefits—who forgives all your sins and heals all your diseases, who redeems your life from the pit and crowns you with love and compassion, who satisfies your desires with good things so that your youth is renewed like the eagle's. Psalm 103:2-5 In the Old Testament, everyone who had committed sin had to bring animal sacrifices.

In the new covenant, Jesus paid for all your sins once and for all. You simply need to receive the benefits of what Jesus did for you.

- Salvation, God forgives all my sin
- Healing, God heals all my diseases
- Redemption, God rescues me from all evil

- Transformation, God puts His love in us
- Provision, God provides everything we need according to His riches in Glory by Christ Jesus.

3. The Laver; The Place of Cleansing and Preparing

Therefore, I urge you, brothers, in view of God's mercy, to offer your bodies as living sacrifices, holy and pleasing to God—this is your spiritual act of worship. Romans 12: 1

The next station in the Tabernacle was a bowl of water where people could wash. Checking your hearts and motives and then surrendering your life to God is an important part of daily prayer. At this stage you may also confess your sins using the ten commandments as check mark to confess your sins and ask for forgiveness.

Here are some ways to keep your heart right with God.

Repent from any known sin.

Offer your body to God:

- Your tongue to speak good and not evil
- Your eyes to see God and the needs of others
- Your ears to be sensitive to His voice
- Your hands to do good to others
- Your feet to walk in God's ways
- Offer your mind to God Philippians 4: 8; Romans 12: 2. Ask God to give you the fruit of the Spirit Galatians 5: 22-23.

4. The Candlestick – The Holy Spirit

The Spirit of the LORD will rest on him—the Spirit of wisdom and of understanding, the Spirit of counsel and of might, the Spirit of the knowledge and fear of the LORD. Isaiah 11: 2

The next in the Tabernacle was a seven-branch golden candlestick. The fire represents the Holy Spirit. Every day you should invite the presence of the Holy Spirit into your life.

- The Spirit of the Lord of Holiness
- The Spirit of Wisdom
- The Spirit of Understanding
- The Spirit of Counsel
- The Spirit of Might
- The Spirit of Knowledge
- The Fear of the Lord

You should also ask the Lord to give you spiritual gifts. 1 Corinthians 12: 8-10

5. The Table of Shewbread – The Word of God

This Book of the Law shall not depart from your mouth, but you[c] shall meditate in it day and night, that you may observe to do according to all that is written in it. For then you will make your way prosperous, and then you will have good success. Joshua 1: 8

A table with twelve loaves of bread represents the importance of reading God's Word for daily sustenance. With this in mind, here are some ways to nourish your soul:

- Read Gods Word.
- Claim His many great promises.
- Ask for fresh revelation from the Word.
- Take time to read and meditate on the Word.
- Get a Word for the day.

6. The Altar of Incense - Worship

The name of the LORD is a strong tower; the righteous run to it and are safe. Proverbs 18: 10

An altar of burning incense stood at the entrance to the Holy of Holies, where God's presence dwelt. This altar represents worship. The people of God literally entered God's presence worshipping the Names of God, including:

- God is My Righteousness – Jeremiah 23: 6
- God is My Sanctifier – Leviticus 20: 7-8
- God is My Healer – Exodus 15: 26
- God is My Provider – Genesis 22: 14
- God is My Banner of Victory – Exodus 17: 15
- God is My Peace – Judges 6: 24
- God is My Shepherd – Psalm 23: 1
- God is Always There – Ezekiel 48: 35

7. The Ark of the Covenant; The Place of Intercession

I urge, then, first of all, that requests, prayers, intercession and thanks-giving be made for everyone—for kings and all those in authority, that we may live peaceful and quiet lives in all godliness and holiness. This is good, and pleases God our Saviour, who wants all men to be saved and to come to a knowledge of the truth. 1 Timothy 2:1-4.

The final place in the Tabernacle was the place where God's presence dwelt. It was there that the priest interceded on behalf of the people. In the New Testament you and I are all called priests and instructed to intercede for others. Those in authority: spiritual, civil, family, and workplace.

The Tabernacle formula in our daily prayers serves as a profound blueprint for approaching God, reflecting the progression from outer worship to intimate communion with Him. Beginning with thanksgiving and praise, symbolized by the Outer Court, it prepares our hearts and aligns our focus on God's greatness. Moving inward, the Holy Place represents deeper engagement through intercession, Scripture meditation, and spiritual reflection, bringing us to a closer relationship with God. Finally, entering the Most Holy Place signifies ultimate intimacy, where we commune with God's presence, aligning our will with His and receiving divine guidance, strength, and revelation. This structured approach will helps you cultivate reverence, focus, and spiritual depth in your daily prayer life.

THE PRAYER OF AGREEMENT

The prayer of agreement is powerful and it helps us to pray more.

"Again I say unto you, That if two of you shall agree on earth as touching anything that they shall ask, it shall be done for them of My Father which is in Heaven." Matthew 18:19

"One can chase one thousand and two chase ten thousand...". "And five of you shall chase an hundred, and an hundred of you shall put ten thousand to flight: and your enemies shall fall before you by the sword." Leviticus 26: 8

Agreement prayer is powerful because it unites believers in faith, aligning their hearts and petitions with God's will. When believers gather in agreement, their combined faith and unity amplify the spiritual impact of their prayers. This type of prayer strengthens relationships, and encourages mutual account-ability, allowing individuals to support one another spiritually. Agreement prayer reflects the unity of the Body of Christ and creates a space for the Holy Spirit to move mightily, bringing about breakthroughs, divine intervention, and answers that glorify God.

We need to be surrounded by dedicated prayer warriors and be humble enough to ask assistance in prayer because demons most of the time come in troops, sometimes in legions; therefore ask The Lord for His spiritual gifts in your life – like discernment of spirits, and to lead you concerning who you should be praying with. Your pastor will be in a better position to help you, and if you are a minister your co-workers are the first choice.

CASTING OUT DEVILS

"And these signs shall follow them that believe; In my name shall they cast out devils; they shall speak with new tongues; 18 They shall take up serpents; and if they drink any deadly thing, it shall not hurt them; they shall lay hands on the sick, and they shall recover". Mark 16: 17-18

The Importance of Discernment in Spiritual Warfare

Engaging in spiritual warfare requires the ability to see, discern, and perceive by the Holy Spirit so as to know what is happening in the spiritual realm. It is vital to be strong in the LORD and in the power of His might to confront such battles effectively. In the meantime, seeking assistance and agreeing in prayer with a seasoned minister is both wise and ideal.

2 Kings 6:17 *"And Elisha prayed, and said, LORD, I pray thee, open his eyes, that he may see. And the LORD opened the eyes of the young man; and he saw: and, behold, the mountain was full of horses and chariots of fire round about Elisha."*

Pray to discern exactly what you are seeing, what is it precisely? The evil spirits disguise and pretend to be what they are not but they cannot deceive the HOLY SPIRIT, therefore pray for discernment of spirits. It is a gift, you need it, you can ask for this gift in prayer and receive it from God. The Church needs people that have the gifts to assist others.

Demons usually employ deceptive strategies, often referred to as "identity tricks," to confuse and manipulate. As liars and deceivers, they follow the cunning nature of their master, satan, whose hallmark is subtlety and subterfuge. These spiritual entities are adept at disguising themselves in ways that seem innocent or familiar. They may appear as young children, beautiful girls, or even take on the form of people we know and trust. This ability to mask their true nature is a deliberate ploy to gain access and wreak havoc in unsuspecting lives.

At times, these entities may manifest in formless, shadowy shapes, but once they infiltrate a person, they take on a distinct presence that can cause emotional, spiritual, and even physical pain. They seek to oppress, distract, and torment. Their ultimate goal is to derail believers from their God-given purpose and cause them to live in bondage. Identifying these spirits is critical because once their identities are exposed, their power diminishes, and they can be cast out in the name of Jesus.

However, spiritual discernment is essential before engaging in direct confrontation. If you are unsure about what you are dealing with in the spirit realm, it is crucial to seek clarity. Rushing into spiritual warfare without a clear understanding of the nature of the opposition can lead to confusion and, in some cases, greater spiritual turmoil.

In moments of uncertainty, turn to the Holy Spirit, who is our divine Counsellor and Guide. Pray fervently in tongues, allowing the Spirit to intercede through you and provide divine insight. The act of praying in tongues connects you directly to the mind of God and empowers you to discern spiritual realities that may not be immediately apparent. As you persist in prayer, the Holy Spirit will illuminate your understanding and confirm what you are confronting.

Once you have received clarity, stand firm in the authority given to you through our Lord Jesus Christ. Command the demonic spirits to leave in His name, declaring His victory over all darkness. Remember that the name of Jesus carries power, and at His name, every knee must bow, both in heaven and on earth and under the earth (Philippians 2:10). With unwavering faith, command the forces of darkness to flee, and they will obey because of the power and authority inherent in Jesus' name.

Spiritual warfare requires both wisdom and boldness. As you grow in prayer and intimacy with God, your ability to discern and overcome the enemy's strategies will be sharpened. Demonic identities may be subtle, but through prayer and the guidance of the Holy Spirit, they will always be revealed, and their hold can be broken.

A Word of Wisdom for Spiritual Warfare

For those engaging in spiritual warfare, particularly in the ministry of casting out demons, it is crucial to handle this responsibility with wisdom and precision.

When commanding demons to leave, it is not sufficient to simply say, "Out!" or "Come out!" While such commands carry authority in the name of Jesus Christ and will compel them to obey, their departure can result in them wandering aimlessly and finding another place to inhabit.

Instead, always direct these spirits with a specific destination in your command. For instance, send them into dry places, back to their senders, into the lake of fire, or into the abyss, as the Holy Spirit leads. This ensures that the spirits are banished to places where they cannot continue their destructive work. This practice is not only scriptural but also strategic, safeguarding the environment and the people involved in the deliverance process.

Remember, demons are legalistic entities that seek open doors or unguarded places to reestablish their influence. Jesus warned in Matthew 12:43-45 about unclean spirits returning to their original habitation if it remains empty, swept, and unguarded. Therefore, it is essential not only to expel demons but also to spiritually fortify the person or place that has been cleansed. Fill the void with the Word of God, prayer, and the presence of the Holy Spirit.

Engaging in spiritual warfare is not a matter to take lightly. It requires wisdom, discernment, and reliance on the Holy Spirit. Be wise in your words and actions, ensuring that you align with God's authority and guidance.

GOD GAVE ME THE SWORD FOR BATTLE AND TOOK AWAY MY CROSS

In the first years of my conversion, I vividly experienced the workings of the Holy Spirit in the spiritual realm. One recurring manifestation was an overwhelming, bright light; a profound and unmistakable sign of His presence. This light would flood my spirit, often accompanied by divine visions, vivid illustrations, and unmistakable guidance that left no room for doubt.

During that season of my walk with God, I discovered that revelations came in various forms: through dreams that unfolded mysteries, Scripture that seemed to leap off the page with meaning, and the gentle yet clear voice of the Holy Spirit whispering His will into my heart. These encounters brought deep comfort and reassurance, reminding me of God's closeness and His active involvement in my life.

Yet, there was a specific and unique period during my spiritual battles when my visions were marked by the repeated appearance of a cross. It would emerge clearly, commanding my attention and anchoring my focus amidst the intensity of those moments. I came to understand this as a divine reminder of Christ's ultimate victory and the power of His sacrifice. The cross seemed to stand as a beacon of hope and authority, reinforcing that no matter how fierce the battle, the victory was already secured through Him.

Looking back, these experiences were not only formative but also profoundly faith-building. They taught me to discern the voice and presence of God, rely on His revelations, and draw strength from the glorious work of Christ.

The appearance of the cross in those moments was a signal of the difficulty and intensity of the battles I faced. It was as though the cross symbolized the weight and tedious nature of the spiritual struggle I was engaged in. This left me puzzled, for I knew that Christ had already borne the cross for me. I began to ask the Lord in prayer, "Father, why do I continue to see this cross in front of me when I am engaged in battle? Didn't Christ carry it on my behalf?"

I brought this question before the Lord repeatedly, seeking clarity. Then, one day, as I was praying; not even about the cross, but about another matter entirely; the Lord surprised me with an extraordinary vision. In this moment, He performed a miraculous act that forever changed the way I approach spiritual warfare.

As I prayed, the cross appeared once again in front of me. But this time, I saw something different happening. The Lord slowly turned the cross upside down. I watched in awe as the cross transformed right before my eyes, its shape shifting until it became a shining sword. The Lord then placed the sword into my right hand, and I heard Him say, "USE IT."

At first, I was astonished and unsure what to do. I looked at the sword in my hand, wondering, "How do I wield this?" Yet, as I stood there, the power of God filled my right hand, and I suddenly found myself moving with confidence. It was as if I had been trained by the Spirit Himself. I began using the sword, slashing through spiritual obstacles and defeating the enemy with precision and strength. I realized that this was no ordinary sword; it was the Sword of the Spirit, the Word of God, empowered by divine authority.

From that day onward, the Lord equipped me with this mighty weapon for spiritual battle. No longer do I see a cross as a symbol of struggle in my visions. Instead, I see the sword firmly in my hand, ready to be used whenever the need arises. When I wield it, I fight with boldness and victory, cutting through the schemes of the enemy and destroying strongholds in the power of the Lord.

This transformation was a profound reminder that Christ has already borne the burden of the cross on our behalf. The battles we face now are not to carry a load that has already been lifted but to take up the sword of victory and conquer in His name. Hallelujah!

When engaging in spiritual warfare, it is essential to understand that even the movements of your hands and body carry significance in the spiritual realm. These physical gestures can be expressions of authority and faith, aligning with the power of the Holy Spirit to bind evil spirits, subdue them, destroy their strongholds, and cast them out into dry places where they cannot cause harm. In the name of Jesus Christ, these actions are established and effective, for His name carries ultimate power and dominion over all darkness.

Evil spirits are relentless and brutal. They are not moved by pleas or gentle requests; rather, they respond to the authority and commands of a believer who knows their identity in Christ. These spirits do not approach for negotiation or compromise; they come with a specific and destructive mission. As Jesus Himself warned in John 10:10, *"The thief cometh not, but for to steal, and to kill, and to destroy: I am come that they might have life, and that they might have it more abundantly."* Understanding their agenda helps us recognize the urgency and intensity with which we must resist them.

The language that evil spirits understand is one of spiritual authority, firm resistance, and the violence of faith. Jesus emphasized this in Matthew 11:12: *"And from the days of John the Baptist until now the kingdom of heaven suffereth violence, and the violent take it by force."* Spiritual warfare demands an unwavering posture of readiness. Whenever the enemy launches an attack, you must stand your ground, armed with the Word of God, and resist him as a soldier. James 4:7 assures us, *"Resist the devil, and he will flee from you."*

Fear has no place in the heart of a believer engaged in spiritual battle. We are not left defenceless, nor are we called to rely on human strength. Instead, we are equipped with divine weapons that are mighty through God. As apostle Paul writes in 2 Corinthians 10:4,

"For the weapons of our warfare are not carnal, but mighty through God to the pulling down of strongholds." These weapons include prayer, fasting, the Word of God, the power of the Holy Spirit, the blood of Jesus, and the power of His name.

Through these spiritual weapons, we pull down strongholds, demolish arguments, and overcome every scheme of the enemy. The authority we wield is not ours alone; it flows from our relationship with Christ, who has already triumphed over principalities and powers, making a public spectacle of them on the cross (Colossians 2:15). Thus, when we confront the enemy, we do so from a position of victory, knowing that the battle belongs to the Lord.

Remember, spiritual warfare is not a one-time event but a continuous fight of faith. The enemy will try to intimidate, distract, and discourage, but as soldiers in God's army, we remain steadfast, vigilant, and victorious.

Through fervent prayer and unwavering trust in God, we enforce His will on earth, take back territory from the enemy, and walk in the abundant life Jesus Christ has promised us.

Night Warfare Prayers

Night prayers are a strategic time for breaking through in the spiritual realm, overcoming and conquering spiritual forces of darkness. These forces are particularly active during the night, making it an opportune moment to engage in spiritual warfare and claim the victory promised by the Lord.

As Elijah called fire from heaven, so can believers invoke the power of the Holy Spirit. The scripture declares in 2 Kings 1:12: *"And Elijah answered and said unto them, If I be a man of God, let fire come down from heaven, and consume thee and thy fifty. And the fire of God came down from heaven, and consumed him and his fifty."* This demonstrates the authority Christians have when walking in faith and obedience.

Christians are equipped with mighty weapons for spiritual battles. During the night, believers can call for divine intervention, using the Sword of the Word of God and the Name of Jesus to gain victory. The Name of Jesus is a powerful force that drives away the enemy, rendering them powerless.

Additionally, the Blood of Jesus serves as a shield, offering protection from attacks and ensuring safety in the midst of the fight.

The night battle is a time to boldly stand in faith, knowing that the weapons of our warfare are not carnal but mighty through God to pull down strongholds. Let us rise with the confidence that we are more than conquerors through Him who loves us.

You can surround yourself and your family with the blazing fire of the Holy Spirit; a divine power that neutralizes the works of the enemy. Call upon the anointing of thunder or invoke the sharp thorns of the Holy Spirit to block and destroy demonic forces, reducing their influence to ashes.

Ask for supernatural strength, like that of Samson, to stand firm in spiritual warfare. As you declare these words in faith, battles are won, and victory is secured in the Name of JESUS.

For greater effectiveness in spiritual battles, pair your prayers with fasting, ensuring your heart is clear of unforgiveness by reconciling with neighbours and family members. During these times of warfare, it's also essential to pray for the Church, interceding for God's work to move forward. In the Name of JESUS, we come against every evil force attempting to hinder the Church, binding them and casting them into dry places.

Worship adds extraordinary power to prayer. Encourage the worship team to sing unto the Holy Spirit, creating an atmosphere that fuels the warriors' prayers and keeps the spiritual atmosphere charged for victory.

Understanding the enemy's tactics is key to overcoming him. Demons operate in shifts, establish covenants, and draw strength from acts of witchcraft such as blood sacrifices, immorality, and perverse practices. Christians must remain steadfast in prayer to dismantle these strategies and render them powerless.

With continuous prayer, fasting, and worship, we walk in the assured victory of JESUS, advancing His Kingdom and silencing every force of darkness.

HOLINESS IS REQUIRED FOR A CHRISTIAN ENGAGING INTO SPIRITUAL WARFARE

When you are clean your prayers have a greater effect.

Psalm 141: 2 (NKJV) *"Let my prayer be set before You as incense,..."* Our prayers rise before God like a pleasant sweet aroma of incense. Perhaps you may think of the aroma of your favourite flower.

Imagine the pleasure that your favourite perfume gives to you. As we pray, as we come before God with trust and especially with the name of Jesus on our lips, our prayers give great pleasure to God. As you offer your prayers to God, in Jesus' name, your prayer comes before Him as a sweet and pleasant aroma. No wonder God loves to answer our prayers. Amen!

On the other hand, in the camp of the enemy our prayers appear like a smoke. They appear to them in three forms:

Weak prayers of sinners appear to them like a light tiny smoke which disappears or vanishes in a little time.

The second level of prayers appears to them like a real smoke, it can reach the covering of demons and then disappears also.

• But the type of prayer that will go like a smoke of fire, it will melt their covering like wax, and consume them, that is the effective prayer. James 5: 16 *"Confess your faults one to another, and pray one for another, that ye may be healed. The effectual fervent prayer of a righteous man availeth much."*

It is good to keep on praying because sometimes as you start, your prayer may be like a weak smoke but as you continue it can turn to thick smoke and as you continue, it turns to thick fiery fire so powerful and it can pierce through their covering or blanket to consume them. when they realise that prayers are about to turn into fire, they send their agents on earth and say: go and distract that person from praying, from focusing. When telephone rings you go and answer it, you are distracted and after the call, you go back to the beginning all over again. The distraction can also be hunger or sleep or pain or all the other symptoms we mentioned earlier on.

we need a strong focused persistence, we need to keep pressing until the fire touches and melts their covering, it is so hot that they all flee, or they are burnt. Then for us at that stage prayer becomes smoother and nicer. God takes care of our time, we continue to pray and there is no resistance anymore, we just continue to flow in the Spirit. The presence of God is felt.

The presence of God is the pillar that upholds our lives. It strengthens and sustains us, breaking the chains of the enemy. In His presence, every bondage is weakened, shattered, and rendered powerless, while the grip of unbelief is completely overcome.

The presence of God is what makes all the difference, and it is the key to effective prayer.

When God's presence fills a place; whether it's a Church or a hall hosting a special program; this creates an atmosphere where deliverance and healing flow freely through His servants. It is during such moments that men and women of God minister powerfully to those in need.

However, those who carry God's presence are often targeted by the enemy, who studies their weaknesses: be it anger, social media distractions, or struggles with purity. The enemy understands that yielding to temptation can hinder their connection with God, disrupting the flow of His presence and power.

Let us pray that God strengthens His servants, shielding them from the enemy's schemes and empowering them to stand firm in His grace. In Jesus' Name, Amen.

You can pray daily, asking the Lord for victory over temptations and protection from any trap of the enemy. I pray that you will be spared from evil, and that the Lord will intervene to deliver you from the evil one. May you experience breakthrough in prayer!

In some cases, evil spirits can hinder the delivery of answers to prayers, as seen in the story of Daniel. Every Christian has angels assigned to them, and these angels carry answers to our prayers. This dynamic is beautifully illustrated in Jacob's dream of a ladder reaching from earth to heaven, with angels ascending and descending on it.

When a Christian is equipped with the full spiritual armour of God, as described in Ephesians 6, answers to prayers can come more easily. However, without the proper spiritual defences: like the helmet of salvation or the shield of faith; angels may face resistance. In spiritual warfare, evil spirits can oppose and overpower angels delivering answers, stealing blessings meant for the believer. This happens particularly when Christians do not persevere in prayer.

All good things come from God, but the devil often seeks to intercept and steal blessings. When angels are hindered, the Christian may be left without their ministering spirits, becoming vulnerable. Over time, the enemy may even send deceptive spirits masquerading as angels of light. These false angels can lead believers into wrong decisions, planting harmful ideas and confusion.

So, how can Christians succeed in this area? The key lies in persistent, faith-filled prayer and the consistent use of God's spiritual armour. By standing firm in prayer and truth, believers can ensure that their blessings are not intercepted and that they remain aligned with God's will.

Using the Armor of God

Ephesians 6: 13-18 exhorts us to: *"Take up the whole armour of God, that you may be able to withstand in the evil day, and having done all, to stand firm. Stand therefore, having girded your waist with truth, having put on the breastplate of righteousness, and having shod your feet with the preparation of the gospel of peace; above all, taking the shield of faith with which you will be able to quench all the fiery darts of the wicked one. Take the helmet of salvation and the sword of the Spirit, which is the word of God; praying always with all prayer and supplication in the Spirit, being watchful to this end with all perseverance and supplication for all the saints."*

This armour fights on our behalf, empowering us to stand victorious against the forces of darkness.

Ministering Angels: Understand and study the role of ministering spirits; angels sent to serve according to the will of God. They operate in alignment with His purpose and not otherwise.

The Role of the Holy Spirit: The Holy Spirit dwells within us as our guide, teacher, and advocate. He stands with us, leading us to pray effectively. We do not command Him in the battle; rather, He uses us as instruments to achieve victory.

When the Holy Spirit prompts you to pray; whether with a simple *"Pray now"* or a specific call to *"fast and pray for a set period of time"* do not delay. He sees the battles ahead and wants to protect you from harm, securing your victory. Obedience to His guidance brings deliverance and triumph. Amen.

CHAPTER 4

PRAYING WITH GOD'S WORD

CHAPTER 4

PRAYING WITH GOD'S WORD

Prayer is the act of communicating with God. It involves declaring His Word and believing in faith that His promises will be fulfilled according to His perfect will.

As Hebrews 11: 3 says:

"Through faith we understand that the worlds were framed by the Word of God, so that things which are seen were not made of things which do appear."

Prayer holds tremendous power; it brings healing to hearts, transformation to lives, and restoration to nations.

Sometimes, all you need is your Bible. Open it and begin to apply the Word of God to your life and to those around you.

- Read of God's Great works.
- Find reasons to give thanks for His goodness and faithfulness.
- Speak the Word of God over your challenges, commanding them to be removed in Jesus' name.
- Use the Word of God in prayer to cast out devils, tear down evil imaginations, and declare victory over every opposition.

Through prayer and the Word of God, you can access God's power and see His hand move mightily in your life. God can accomplish extraordinary things through your prayers.

The Bible declares in Jeremiah 1:9–10:

"Then the LORD reached out His hand, touched my mouth, and said to me, 'Behold, I have put My words in your mouth. See, I have this day set you over nations and kingdoms, to uproot and tear down, to destroy and overthrow, to build and to plant.'"

HOW TO PRAY WITH THE WORD OF GOD?

Choose a meaningful passage: Begin by selecting a Scripture that resonates deeply with you and speaks to your life in this moment.

Prepare your heart: Ask God to bless your time in His Word, to keep your mind focused, and to guide you as you pray through Scripture.

Meditate on the passage: Read slowly, reflecting on each word and verse. Allow the truths of the passage to sink into your heart.

Pray through the Word: As you read, turn the ideas and truths of the passage into personal prayers, bringing your thoughts and needs before God.

Glorify God: Use your time with Scripture to magnify His name and let His Word uplift and encourage your spirit.

Practical Example: Praying with the Book of Genesis

Let's see how we can apply this approach, beginning with the Book of Genesis. Start with Genesis chapters 1 through 7. Genesis, the Book of Beginnings, is profoundly inspiring. It invites us to humble ourselves, seek to know God more intimately, and commit to obeying Him.

Genesis reveals God as the Creator and the Ultimate Leader of all things. He is The Good Father, whose mercies endure forever. By praying through these chapters, you can draw closer to God, reflecting on His Character, Creation, and Covenant.

For example:

Genesis 1: Praise God as the Creator of all things, acknowledging His power and creativity. Pray for His order and light to fill your life just as He brought order to creation.

Genesis 2: Thank God for His provision and design for human relationships. Pray for wisdom in your stewardship of His blessings.

Genesis 3: Confess areas of weakness, asking God for forgiveness and restoration where sin has caused separation.

Genesis 6-7: Reflect on Noah's obedience and faith. Ask God for grace to walk faithfully with Him, even in challenging times.

This method of praying through Scripture can be applied to any book of the Bible. With this approach, you will never run out of words in prayer. God's Word becomes your guide, ensuring that your prayers are aligned with His will and His promises.

I thank You, Lord, for being my Creator, the One who, in the beginning, made the heavens and the earth (*Genesis 1: 1*).

If my life feels void and without form, let Your Spirit hover over me, bringing light and order. Let every shadow and darkness in my life yield to Your radiant light, shaping me according to Your perfect will, in the name of Jesus Christ (*Genesis 1: 2*).

Father, make my life fruitful, causing it to bear good and lasting fruits for Your glory.

You created me to have dominion over all Your creation (*Genesis 1: 26, 28*). Lord, keep me centred in Your will. Grant me the wisdom and strength to walk in the authority You have given, never letting creation dominate me.

Lord, deliver me from the bondage of my fallen nature. Redeem me by the power of Your grace and the blood of Jesus Christ, which breaks the chains of sin.

I surrender my life to You, Lord. I desire not to live for myself but as a living sacrifice for You. Teach me to follow Your lead, obey Your voice, and honour You all my days.

Lord, establish Your covenant of rest and sanctification with me. As You sanctified the seventh day, let me cease from needless striving and walk in Your peace, fulfilling only always what is pleasing in Your sight (*Genesis 2: 2-3*).

Father, let Your holy mist fall upon my life, refreshing and nourishing me so that I may flourish. Breathe into me the breath of life, that I may become a vessel of abundant life to others (*Genesis 2: 6-7*).

Plant within me a garden of Godliness. Let it grow and flourish with trees that are good and pleasing, bearing fruits of righteousness. (*Genesis 2: 8*).

Let the river of life flow through me, Lord. May it branch into streams that bring living water to the thirsty souls around me, in the name of Jesus Christ (*Genesis 2: 10*).

Make me just and blameless in this generation Lord, and teach me to walk faithfully with You all my days (*Genesis 6: 9*). Empower me with a life of virtue and righteousness that brings delight to Your heart.

"Now the earth was corrupt in God's sight..." (Genesis 6: 11) I declare: Every power of corruption working against me, perish now! I will not be corrupt, my children will not be corrupt, and my spouse will not be corrupt on this earth. I stand firmly against the spirit of corruption and cover my family with the precious blood of Jesus Christ.

"God saw how corrupt the earth had become..." (Genesis 6: 12) Corruption of the earth, I renounce you! I will not corrupt my ways; instead, I choose to be the light of the world and the salt of the earth, standing against all forms of corruption in the mighty Name of Jesus Christ. Deliver me, Lord, from the violence of men, and protect me from harm.

Lord, I pray, shield my family and me in Your Ark of safety, just as You sheltered Noah with gopher wood and pitch against the rains of life. *"So make yourself an ark of cypress wood; make rooms in it and coat it with pitch inside and out."* (Genesis 6: 14)

"But I will establish my covenant with you..." (Genesis 6:18) Establish Your covenant of good health, long life, and salvation with me, my spouse, and my children, Lord. Let us walk in Your promises, in the mighty Name of Jesus Christ.

Provide for us abundantly, Lord, according to Your Word. Let my family never lack any good thing. *"You are to take every kind of food that is to be eaten and store it away as food for you and for them."* (Genesis 6: 21)

Grant me the power and wisdom to obey You wholeheartedly, Lord. Help me to walk in alignment with Your will. *"Noah did everything just as God commanded him."* (Genesis 6: 22)

Set me apart, Lord, and make me righteous in this generation. Keep me from sinning against You in any way, and help me to live a life that honours You. *"The Lord then said to Noah, 'Go into the ark, you and your whole family, because I have found you righteous in this generation.'"* (Genesis 7: 1)

Cleanse me, Lord, both inwardly and outwardly, by the blood of the Lamb. Let my household also be saved from the corruption of the world in the Name of my Lord Jesus Christ. (Genesis 7: 7)

Lord, just as You spared Noah, Your servant, and his family from the floodwaters, I pray that You will also spare me and my family from the storms of life. (Genesis 7: 13-16, 23)

Spare me, Lord, so that I may fulfil all that You have called me to do, in the Name of my Lord Jesus Christ.

In Your loving kindness, in Your power of deliverance, remember me, Father. In Your power of salvation, in Your power of multiplication, in Your power of favour, remember me, Lord. In Your healing power, remember me, Lord, so that Your Name may be glorified in my life, Father.

May the Lord quicken your prayer life by the creative power of His Word, in the Name of Jesus Christ. Amen.

Let's Continue to Pray with Other Scriptures

Ephesians 1:15–23 This passage contains one of the powerful prayers in Scripture. As we meditate on it, let's apply it to our lives for the next nine months; the time it takes to incubate and birth something new. As you pray these verses over yourself, you will witness transformation. A new version of yourself will emerge, filled with possibilities. You'll look back and marvel, wondering if you had truly experienced God's power before this journey.

Starting from verse 17, the focus of the prayer is clear:

"That the God of our Lord Jesus Christ, the Father of glory, may give to you the spirit of wisdom and revelation in the knowledge of Him, the eyes of your understanding being enlightened; that you may know what is the hope of His calling, what are the riches of the glory of His inheritance in the saints, and what is the exceeding greatness of His power toward us who believe, according to the working of His mighty power." (Ephesians 1:17–19, NKJV)

Let's unpack this powerful prayer into three key points:

1. The Hope of Your Calling

Pray that God will open your eyes to understand the hope of your calling. This means knowing your divine purpose; the reason God created you and called you in Christ. When you pray with wisdom and revelation, you begin to understand your place in God's grand design.

2. The Riches of His Inheritance in the Saints

This prayer asks for revelation of the riches of God's inheritance in us, His saints. Pray to grasp what you mean to God and to understand the rights, privileges, and treasures you have in Christ.

3. The Greatness of His Power

Pray to experience the exceeding greatness of God's power toward you as a believer. This is the same power that raised Christ from the dead and seated Him in heavenly places, far above all principality, power, might, and dominion. This power is at work in you! As you pray, ask God to reveal how His mighty power can manifest in your life.

How to Pray Using This Passage

Open your Bible and pray through the verses line by line. Personalize it. Insert your name, the names of your loved ones, your husband, children, or the brethren in your assembly.

Pray in your understanding and in the Spirit.

Meditate on the words and let the Holy Spirit guide you deeper into their meaning.

Example:

"Father, I pray that You give me, the Spirit of wisdom and revelation in the knowledge of You. Enlighten the eyes of my understanding so that I may know the hope of Your calling in my life. Reveal to me the riches of

Your inheritance in me and the greatness of Your power working in and through me. Let this power bring transformation in every area of my life."

As you consistently pray this prayer, your spiritual eyes will open to see God's plans and purposes for your life. The transformation will not only impact you but also those around you. Persist in prayer, and watch God move mightily!

Two major sources guide us in praying effectively: the Scriptures and the Holy Spirit. The Scriptures are a wellspring of prayers, while the Holy Spirit often inspires songs and messages that align with God's Word.

One way to deeply internalize God's Word is to turn both the Scriptures and the messages we hear into songs. When you sing a prayer or a message, it lingers in your heart and mind long after the words are spoken.

Repeating the prayer as a song solidifies it in memory, making it part of your daily worship. You can even create stanzas for different prayer points, drawing directly from the message preached. When this becomes a weekly practice, turning sermons into songs, it ensures the Word is not just heard but meditated on and retained.

Let's look at another powerful passage, **Ephesians 3:14–21**, which offers profound prayers:

"For this reason I bow my knees to the Father of our Lord Jesus Christ, From whom the whole family in heaven and earth is named,

That He would grant you, according to the riches of His glory,

To be strengthened with might through His Spirit in the inner man,

That Christ may dwell in your hearts through faith; That you, being rooted and grounded in love, May be able to comprehend with all the saints What is the width and length and depth and height; To know the love of Christ which passes knowledge; That you may be filled with all the fullness of God. Now to Him who is able to do exceedingly abundantly above all that we ask or think, according to the power that works in us, to Him be glory in the church by Christ Jesus to all generations, forever and ever. Amen."

From this passage, we can identify three key prayer points:

Strengthened in the inner man: Pray to be empowered by the Spirit, becoming a strong, unshakable Christian.

Rooted and grounded in love: Pray for a deep foundation in love, so you can forgive and love others freely, strengthening relationships and marriages.

Comprehend the dimensions of God's love: Pray for the ability to grasp the breadth, length, depth, and height of Christ's love, a love that surpasses knowledge.

This prayer reminds us that the fullness of God dwells in Christ, and through Him, we are made complete. When you pray these Scriptures, you align yourself with God's promises and purposes, allowing His Spirit to transform your life.

Let us embrace these prayers, turning them into both declarations and songs, allowing the Word to dwell richly within us and bear fruit for God's glory.

Praying God's Word

The Bible teaches us that the fullness of God dwells in Christ, and through Him, we are made complete. Prayer brings us into that place of completeness in God. When we pray God's Word, it strengthens us and aligns our lives with His purposes.

Let's consider four key aspects to pray into your life, and as you do, remember to pray for others too. Lift your voice and pray with the Scriptures open before you. Don't just look at your phone; open your Bible and actively engage with the Word. Pray for yourself, and pray specifically to be strengthened with might by His Spirit in your inner man.

The "inner man" is the real you, the spirit that must gain strength to ascend and dominate your whole being. Without this spiritual strength, we remain weak and spiritually ineffective. The Bible says that only those strengthened by the Spirit can prevail, and it is through prayer that this strength comes.

Declare it in faith:

"Lord, strengthen me with might by Your Spirit in my inner man. Oh God, I pray that Christ may dwell in my heart by faith, so that I may truly know the hope of His calling."

This aligns with Philippians 1: 6, which says:

"Being confident of this, that He who began a good work in you will carry it on to completion until the day of Christ Jesus."

Let this truth resonate in your heart. Pray with confidence:

"God, You have begun a good work in me. Complete it, perfect it, and bring it to full conclusion in Your time. Do not let me falter or go astray.

Work in me both to will and to do Your good pleasure. Let the work You started in me grow, continue, and be perfected until the day of Christ Jesus. I cooperate with the Holy Spirit as He works in me. I desire to grow daily in Your likeness through studying, listening to, memorizing, and meditating on Your Word. Complete the good work in me as I yield to You."

This prayer brings us into deeper alignment with God's will, shaping us to be ambassadors of heaven, walking in His purpose.

Even the songs we sing are often birthed from Scripture. For example, Philippians 1: 6 inspired believers to craft songs of faith and confidence:

"Being confident of this very thing, that He who began a good work in me shall perform it until the day of Christ Jesus."

As you pray and meditate on these truths, allow the Scriptures to inspire not only your prayers but also songs of worship that flow from a heart filled with God's Word. Every Scripture carries a message of hope and transformation, waiting to be prayed, sung, and lived out.

Amen.

Praying God's Word: Philippians 1: 9-11

"And this I pray, that your love may abound still more and more in knowledge and all discernment, that you may approve the things that are excellent, that you may be sincere and without offense till the day of Christ, being filled with the fruits of righteousness which are by Jesus Christ, to the glory and praise of God." (Philippians 1: 9-11, NKJV)

These verses are a powerful prayer for growth in love, discernment, Godliness, and righteousness: This prayer has three main requests:

1. Growth in Love

The first request is for an *abounding love*, a love that increases continually in knowledge and discernment. It's a call to grow in compassion and kindness, toward God and toward others. For instance, if you previously helped three people, let your love motivate you to help twice as much or more. This growth in love reflects in how you treat your spouse, your neighbours, and everyone around you. It's about becoming more Christlike in love.

2. Living with Godly Discernment and Integrity

The second request asks that believers may *approve things that are excellent*; that is, to discern and choose what pleases God. Praying for sincerity and living without offense, ensuring our lives honour Christ. This involves praying for a Godly character, where hypocrisy has no place. Christians should strive to please God, not grieve Him.

Transformation in our Christian walk comes through studying the Word, hearing the Word, and praying. These practices plant the seeds of growth in our lives. And when we persist, we'll be amazed at how our spiritual lives flourish.

3. Bearing the Fruits of Righteousness

To be *filled with the fruits of righteousness*; a life that glorifies God through good works and Godly character. Jesus Christ tells us, *"Let your light so shine before men, that they may see your good works and glorify your Father in Heaven"* (Matthew 5:16). These good works: winning souls, acts of kindness, and living righteously are fruits that bring glory to God.

This also links to the fruits of the Spirit (Galatians 5:22-23), which reflect Godly character. As love abounds in increasing measure, it will overflow in our actions, decisions, and interactions.

Application

Let's make this personal. Pray that:

1. Your love for God and others will increase and abound more and more in knowledge and discernment.
2. You'll have the wisdom to approve what pleases God and live a life of sincerity and integrity without offense.
3. Your life will be filled with fruits of righteousness that glorify God and reflect His beauty to the world.

This prayer is about transformation; becoming a believer who walks in dominion, whose words carry authority, and whose life demonstrates the power of God. As your love grows, your actions will bring praise and glory to God.

When we pray, we must focus on God's will in all aspects of life; our decisions, relationships, work ethic, and character.

As Philippians 1:10-11 teaches, we should "approve things that are excellent" and strive to have an excellent spirit. This means rejecting mediocrity, avoiding shady dealings, and pursuing what is right, just, and pleasing to God.

Developing a Christlike character that is sincere and without offense is essential. We are called to walk as Christ walked, living a life marked by righteousness, integrity, and strength of character.

When we align our lives with God's Word, we find ourselves in the right place, at the right time, with the right people, doing the right things in the right way. This is the essence of righteousness; living in harmony with God's Will. Thank You, Father, for this privilege. We give You praise, in Jesus' name.

Let us now reflect on the prayers in **Colossians 1: 9-14**, which contain powerful lessons.

"For this cause we also, since the day we heard it, do not cease to pray for you, and to desire that you might be filled with the knowledge of His will in all wisdom and spiritual understanding; that you might walk worthy of The Lord unto all pleasing, being fruitful in every good work, and increasing in the knowledge of God; strengthened with all might, according to His glorious power, unto all patience and long-suffering with joyfulness; giving thanks unto The Father, Who has qualified us to be partakers of the inheritance of the saints in light. He has delivered us from the power of darkness and has translated us into the Kingdom of His dear Son, in Whom we have redemption through His blood, even the forgiveness of sins."

Three major prayer points emerge from this passage:

1. Be filled with the knowledge of His will

Pray for wisdom and spiritual understanding to know God's will for your life. We must seek clarity and direction from God. What is His purpose for you? What steps should you take next?

Pray for insight and discernment to walk in alignment with His divine plan.

2. Walk worthy of the Lord

Pray to live a life that pleases God, bearing fruit in every good work and growing in the knowledge of Him. This involves cultivating Godly character and producing spiritual fruit; love, joy, peace, patience, kindness, and more. For those who are married, for example, you are called to bring joy and peace into your spouse's life. Likewise, our relationship with our Lord Jesus Christ should reflect this devotion and commitment.

3. Be strengthened with His power

Ask for strength to endure with patience and joy, giving thanks to the Father for the gift of salvation. It is through His glorious power that we are enabled to persevere and remain steadfast.

The Church needs a transformation in its prayer life. Many prayers today focus on material needs or defeating enemies, which is good but we should not neglect the deeper matters that shape our walk with God. If we shift our focus to the kind of prayers outlined in Scripture; prayers for spiritual growth, wisdom, and Godly character; we will experience transformational Christianity. The power of such prayers is unmatched, as they align us with God's heart and purpose, giving us victory as well.

Let us return to the Word and pray as the early Church did, allowing Scripture to guide and inspire our prayers. This is how we grow, bear fruit, and become who we are called to be in Christ.

Praying God's Word

When you prioritize prayer and align your focus with God's will, your attention begins to shift from worldly concerns: your career, finances, and personal ambitions; to His purposes. Once you've placed these essential matters before God, you can trust Him to provide for your daily needs, as promised in His Word. This trust allows the power of God to work in your life, strengthening you with might according to His glorious power (Colossians 1:11).

But the power of God is not limited to external manifestations like anointing, healing, or miracles. It also includes an inner strength that equips you to overcome tribulations. This inner strength builds spiritual capacity, resilience under pressure, and endurance through challenges. It enables you to face difficulties without giving up, cultivating patience. These qualities reflect the true power of God at work within you.

Apostle Paul's prayer in Colossians 1:9-10 captures this beautifully: *"That you may be filled with the knowledge of His will in all wisdom and spiritual understanding; that you may walk worthy of the Lord, fully pleasing Him, being fruitful in every good work and increasing in the knowledge of God."*

This prayer emphasizes a life of discipline and character that pleases God. Such fruitfulness requires commitment to studying the Word, meditating on it, and allowing it to transform your understanding. By doing so, you grow in the knowledge of God, which is foundational for knowing and doing His will.

As you pray for strength in your inner being, you are asking to be strengthened with all might according to His glorious power, enabling you to endure with patience and joy. This strength prevents you from faltering in your walk with God. Therefore, we pray for resilience, knowing that through God's strength, we can stand firm.

In summary, four key prayers you can incorporate into your daily intercession:

Ephesians 1:17-19 – Pray for the Spirit of wisdom and revelation in the knowledge of God.

Ephesians 3:16-19 – Pray for strength in your inner being and to comprehend the vast love of Christ.

Colossians 1:9-11 – Pray for wisdom, spiritual understanding, and strength with patience and joy.

Philippians 1:9-11 – Pray for abounding love, discernment, and fruitfulness in righteousness.

Additionally, remember the call in **Ephesians 6:18**: *"Praying always with all prayer and supplication in the Spirit, being watchful to this end with all perseverance and supplication for all the saints."*

Prayer isn't just for yourself. Pray for your family, your brothers and sisters in Christ, and your pastors and leaders. Make it a daily practice to pray for others as you open the Bible and intercede for their needs. Genuine Christianity is reflected in this shared spiritual journey of prayer, support, and mutual growth.

By dedicating time to these prayers and keeping watch for one another, you cultivate a deeper relationship with God, rooted in His Word and empowered by His Spirit

Praying God's Word

When we pray, we desire to see our brothers and sisters grow into what God has called them to be. Prayer is essential in this process. While the preacher plants the seed: The Word of God, it is the intercessors who water it with prayer. They are the ones who create the spiritual environment for growth and transformation. It is God, who ultimately brings the increase and brings about lasting change.

The Apostle Paul reminds us of this truth. In **Ephesians 6:18**, he encourages us to pray "for all the Lord's people." But Paul doesn't stop there. In the next verse (**Ephesians 6:19**), he makes a personal request: *"Pray also for me, that whenever I speak, words may be given me so that I will fearlessly make known the mystery of the gospel."* This is a powerful reminder of the need to pray for our spiritual leaders.

When we gather for service and hear a pastor address specific questions or needs in our hearts, we are witnessing divine utterance at work. The clarity, boldness, and anointing don't happen by chance; it is the result of prayer. Prayer is what transforms a speaker into an oracle of God. It is what sets apart a sermon inspired by the Holy Spirit from a mere lecture. The Church should continually pray for their leaders to receive divine utterance, revelation, and the courage to boldly proclaim God's Word.

Paul emphasizes this further in Ephesians 6:20, saying, *"for which I am an ambassador in chains. Pray that I may declare it fearlessly, as I should."* This highlights the need to pray not only for the message but also for the messengers; so they can speak with boldness and clarity despite opposition.

HOW TO PRAY FOR YOUR PASTORS AND LEADERS

When you pray for your pastor or leader; what should you pray for?

Pray for the Word to have free course in them In **2 Thessalonians 3: 1,** Paul writes, *"Finally, brethren, pray for us, that the Word of the Lord may have free course and be glorified, even as it is with you."* Pray that the message God has entrusted to them will reach its destination unhindered. Pray for it to bear fruit; transforming lives, families, and nations.

1. Pray for their protection

Paul continues in **2 Thessalonians 3: 2,** *"And that we may be delivered from unreasonable and wicked men; for all men have not faith."* Many spiritual leaders face opposition from people who resist the Gospel. It's vital to pray for their safety and deliverance from harmful schemes.

2. Pray for divine utterance

Ask God to grant them boldness, clarity, and the ability to communicate the mysteries of the Gospel effectively. Pray for a fresh anointing that enables them to minister with power and purpose.

The work of the ministry is not a solo endeavour. As members of the Body of Christ, we are called to intercede for those who lead us. Through our prayers, we can help create an atmosphere where God's Word runs swiftly and His purposes are fulfilled. Let us commit to praying for our leaders; so they can continue to serve as vessels of God's grace, truth, and power.

PRAYING GOD'S WORD FOR SAFETY AND DELIVERANCE

The story of Peter's miraculous escape from prison in Acts 12 reveals an important truth: God works in partnership with His people. When James, one of the twelve apostles, was arrested and beheaded by Herod, the Church remained passive, perhaps assuming that God would intervene without their involvement. However, when Peter was arrested, the Church finally woke up and prayed fervently. It was through their united prayers that Peter was delivered from prison, as God sent an angel to break his chains and lead him out.

This account illustrates a critical principle: God requires our active participation. Prayer must be accompanied by faith, initiative, and action.

Advancing the Kingdom of God means confronting the forces of darkness. This is spiritual warfare, and it is not to be taken lightly. Those who preach the gospel are often targeted because they are pulling people out of the kingdom of darkness, we need to pray for them.

The Role of the Church in Supporting Ministers

One weakness in many churches, especially in regions, is the over-reliance on pastors. Believers often say, "Pastor, pray for me," or "Pastor will pray for me," without realizing that they, too, have a responsibility to pray, not just for themselves but also for their leaders.

This is why the Church must rise to its responsibility to pray for the leaders. No general can win a battle without an army.

Similarly, no pastor or minister can fulfil their calling effectively without the support of a praying Church. The relationship between ministers and the congregation is symbiotic: leaders pour out their lives in service, while the congregation supports them through prayer, encouragement, and resources.

The treasure, anointing, wisdom, and power are divine, but the vessel carrying it is human. The Church must uphold them in prayer. As the body of Christ, we share the responsibility for the success of God's work. God has established systems and principles to achieve His purposes, and we are part of that system. Let us be faithful in prayer, recognizing that we are co-labourers with Christ in advancing His Kingdom.

THE HOLY SPIRIT INTERCEDES FOR US

The ministry of the Holy Spirit in prayer is profound and essential. When words are few, the Spirit steps in. When our understanding is limited, He prays beyond human intellect, aligning our petitions with God's divine purposes. His intercession is not based on human reasoning but on the mind of God, ensuring that our prayers are effective and powerful.

The Holy Spirit

- Helps us in our weakness when we do not know how to pray.
- Intercedes with groanings too deep for words.
- Aligns our prayers with God's will, producing divine results.
- Leads us into deeper intimacy with the Father.

As we learn to yield to the Holy Spirit in prayer, we enter into a supernatural realm where our prayers are no longer limited by human effort but are empowered by God Himself. This divine partnership transforms our prayer life, strengthens our faith, and releases God's purposes on the earth.

In the context of the gifts of the Spirit, the word of wisdom, word of knowledge, and prophecy are distinct but interconnected spiritual gifts given by the Holy Spirit for the edification of the Church. Here's a breakdown of each:

1. Word of Wisdom (1 Corinthians 12: 8)

This is a supernatural impartation of divine wisdom for a specific situation.

It is not natural wisdom gained through experience or study but a divinely inspired solution or insight that aligns with God's will.

Example: In Acts 15: 13-21, James received a word of wisdom during the Jerusalem Council, helping resolve the debate about Gentile believers.

2. Word of Knowledge (1 Corinthians 12: 8)

This is a revelation of specific facts or knowledge about a person, situation, or event that could not be known naturally.

It is often given to expose, confirm, or direct something hidden, leading to repentance, healing, or guidance.

Example: In John 4: 16-19, Jesus told the Samaritan woman about her five husbands, revealing knowledge beyond human understanding.

3. Prophecy (1 Corinthians 12: 10; 1 Corinthians 14: 3-4)

This is a Spirit-inspired message spoken for edification, exhortation, and comfort.

It can reveal God's heart, declare His purposes, or sometimes foretell future events (though not always predictive).

Example: In Acts 11: 27-28, Agabus prophesied about a coming famine, allowing the Church to prepare.

Though distinct, these gifts often operate together. For instance, a prophetic word may contain a word of knowledge (revealing something) and a word of wisdom (giving direction on what to do).

More about the Holy Spirit and His Works I will refer you to my book: *The Holy Spirit*.

CHAPTER 5

THE LORD'S PRAYER AS A PATTERN

THE LORD'S PRAYER AS A PATTERN

THE LORD'S PRAYER: A MODEL FOR EFFECTIVE PRAYER

The Lord Jesus Christ exemplified a life of prayer. He consistently communed with The Father, modelling the importance of regular and fervent prayer. It was through His own prayer life that He demonstrated how we, as believers, should approach God. The ultimate expression of His teaching on prayer is encapsulated in what we know as *The Lord's Prayer*, a perfect framework for effective and meaningful prayer.

When the disciples asked the Lord Jesus, *"Lord, teach us to pray"* (Luke 11: 1), His response wasn't a series of vague principles, but rather, a structured prayer; one that provides us with a template to align our hearts and requests with the will of God. The Lord's Prayer addresses every area of our relationship with God, highlighting key aspects of how we should approach Him in humility, submission, and faith.

THE PATTERN OF CONTINUOUS PRAYER

The Lord Jesus didn't just suggest that we pray occasionally or in moments of distress, rather He urged us to pray continuously: *"pray without ceasing"* (1 Thessalonians 5:17). This means that prayer should not be only confined to specific times of the day, but should be an integral and ongoing part of our lives. In the same way, the Lord's Prayer is a template that can be used as part of our continuous prayer, touching on everything from worship and surrender to requests and forgiveness.

Philippians 4:6-7 further encourages us: *"Be anxious for nothing, but in everything by prayer and supplication, with thanksgiving, let your requests be made known to God; and the peace of God, which surpasses all understanding, will guard your hearts and minds through Christ Jesus."*

When we speak of prayer, many Christians may quickly respond, "I pray every day." But the question you must ask yourselves is: Do you really pray enough?

If the Church truly was devoted to prayer as we are called to, the impact of our prayers would be far more evident in the world today.

The power of prayer would transform not just our individual lives but entire communities and nations.

Let us take a moment to reflect on this matter together. We need to carefully examine our approach to prayer, especially in light of the example given by the Lord's Prayer.

Are we praying as we ought to?

Are our prayers aligned with God's will, full of faith, persistence, and sincerity?

By exploring these questions, we can ensure that our daily communication with God is not just a routine, but a powerful, lifechanging encounter with the Divine.

Let us strive to pray more earnestly, understanding that through prayer, we connect with the Almighty, receive His peace, the blessings, and bring His will to be done on earth.

THE LORD'S PRAYER SERVES AS OUR GUIDE IN SCRIPTURE WHEN IT COMES TO PRAYER.

We do not only need to recite this prayer but we can follow the steps of the prayer Word by Word to make sure our prayer requests are covered daily.

The Lord's Prayer originated from a request made by the disciples to The Lord Jesus, asking, "Lord, teach us to pray."

Many Christians today may have the same concerns that the disciples had, wondering if their prayers are effective, if they are praying the right way, or even if their prayers are being presented well before God. It's a common question: "Am I praying enough, and am I praying correctly?" These doubts can lead to a desire for guidance in our prayer life, just as the disciples asked for guidance when they approached Jesus.

In response to their request, Jesus gave them the prayer that we now call the Lord's Prayer, a powerful and timeless model for communicating with God. For many of us, this prayer has become a daily routine. In our household, we recite it every day, and we have taught it to our children, who also pray it regularly. But at one point, the Lord began to reveal to me a deeper understanding of this prayer. He expanded its meaning in my spirit and showed me that there was more to the Lord's Prayer than simply reciting the words. Through this revelation, He led me to write down insights and explanations, revealing the profound depth and detailed structure of the prayer. These clarifications showed how the Lord's Prayer could serve as a comprehensive guide to daily prayer, far beyond mere repetition.

Before turning this understanding into a book, I first shared it as a teaching at our church. After the message, a brother from the university approached me. He admitted that when I announced I would be teaching on the Lord's Prayer, he didn't quite understand why it was necessary. He had always thought of it as something simple and straightforward. But after hearing the message, he said, "I now understand it so much better. Thank you." This response confirmed for me that there is so much more to the Lord's Prayer than meets the eye, and that it holds powerful lessons for anyone seeking to deepen their prayer life.

I said to him, "I simply do my best to obey God, and today He has directed me to preach on this particular prayer." He responded with gratitude, and I replied, "You're welcome, my brother. I'm glad to hear that you understand the significance of the message today. Praise the Lord."

Later that same day, a mother approached me and said, "Thank you for shedding more light on this prayer. I've been praying it since my youth, but today, I feel as though God used you to help me see it in a deeper way. The new insights you provided have allowed me to connect it more meaningfully to my personal prayer life. Thank you for that."

I was humbled by her words, realizing how God's timing and wisdom had touched her through the message. It reminded me that the power of the Lord's Prayer isn't just in its repetition but in the understanding of its deeper meaning. We can live out its truths in our everyday relationship with God, and that is where the true transformation happens. Praise be to God for His guidance and for opening our hearts to His word.

Now, let us see Matthew 6: 9-13 (NKJV).

"In this manner, therefore, pray: **Our Father in heaven, Hallowed be Your name***."*

Starting with these first words *"Our Father in heaven";* I recall a time in our local church in Maastricht when many members seemed dissatisfied, despite all our efforts to serve and care for them. I found myself asking the Lord, "Why are these people not content with all that we do for them?"

The Lord responded clearly, "Try to be like a mother to them, not just a sister or a pastor. Approach them with discipline, parenting skills, love, and prayer, just as you would with your own children at home. Many of them have never experienced or seen a strong mother figure, and they are looking to you to know what it feels like to have a mother. Don't consider their age; simply be a mother to them, and you will notice the difference."

The Lord further revealed to me, "I am not only their God, but I am their Father. When My people see Me as their Father, they feel more secure, more attended to, more blessed, and deeply loved. I have sent you to be My ambassador to them. Do what I am asking of you."

This reminded me of the passage in Jeremiah 3:19: *"But I said, 'How shall I put thee among the children and give thee a pleasant land, a goodly heritage of the hosts of nations?' And I said, 'Thou shalt call Me, My Father, and shalt not turn away from Me.'"*

This powerful instruction from the Lord showed me that just as He is a Father to His people, He was calling me to embody a motherly presence in our community—a role that goes beyond titles or positions. By embracing this approach, I could truly make a difference in the lives of those who looked to me for guidance, comfort, and support.

2 Corinthians 6:18 *"And will be a Father unto you, and ye shall be my sons and daughters, saith the Lord Almighty."*

Since that time, I started to place discipline, regulations, to set time for one to one conversations, sending personal messages of encouragement instead of just group messages, looking at them in the face to give instructions when needed, making more personal prayers with each; spending more time with them when necessary, praying more with them. Making more provision for snacks after service for them and a lot more. I mean I just started strictly and firmly leading it and all of a sudden, to my amazement and admiration they began to redress and honour God in all we did in Church, even to take responsibility to do more activities in Church and actually assist one another. An absolute great difference.

One of the major challenges in churches today is that some leaders, because Christ has made us all one and equal, feel compelled to simply follow the will of the people in order to win their love and respect. However, when church leaders truly embrace their role as spiritual parents, teaching, instructing, loving, praying for their members, defending them, and leading them like fathers and mothers in the faith, there will be greater discipline and, ultimately, more success in the church. People need to feel that they are genuinely cared for.

When studying **God The Father**, especially when seeking to understand Him more deeply, it is essential to repeatedly read the explanation, clarification, and description of the **One** seated on the Throne in Heaven, as revealed in the Book of Revelation. 4: 2-11 "*And immediately I was in the Spirit: and, behold, a throne was set in heaven, and ONE sat on the throne. And He that sat was to look upon like a jasper and a sardine stone: and there was a rainbow round about the throne, in sight like unto an emerald. And round about the throne were four and twenty seats: and upon the seats I saw four and twenty elders sitting, clothed in white raiment; and they had on their heads crowns of gold. And out of the throne proceeded lightnings and thunderings and voices: and there were seven lamps of fire burning before the throne, which are the seven Spirits of God. And before the throne there was a sea of glass like unto crystal: and in the midst of the throne, and round about the throne, were four beasts full of eyes before and behind. And the first beast was like a lion, and the second beast like a calf, and the third beast had a face as a man, and the fourth beast was like a flying eagle. And the four beasts had each of them six wings about him; and they were full of eyes within: and they rest not day and night, saying, Holy, Holy, Holy, LORD God Almighty, which was, and is, and is to come. And when those* *beasts give glory and honour and thanks to him that sat on the throne, who liveth for ever and ever, The four and twenty elders fall down before him that sat on the throne, and worship him that liveth for ever and ever, and cast their crowns before the throne, saying, Thou art worthy, O Lord, to receive glory and honour and power: for Thou hast created all things, and for Thy pleasure they are and were created."*

Amazing!!

Because God is omnipresent, He is everywhere universally at the same time. Residing inside of us by the Person of The Holy Spirit Through Jesus Christ. He is always with us.

Matthew 1: 23 says: *"Behold, a virgin shall be with child, and shall bring forth a Son, and they shall call His name Emmanuel, which being interpreted is,* **God with us".** This verse amazes me every time whenever I read it, because it reminds me that God came actually, truly to be with us by Jesus Christ. So loving and affectionate words: God with us!!

Hallowed means Sanctified, consecrated, highly venerated, Holy; belonging to and deriving from divine Power. In other words, with so much reverence that when the Name of The Lord is mentioned, everybody should bow and worship Him aloud without fear.

Nowadays the persecution against the Church and against the Name of The Lord is so widespread that many Christians find it hard even to reverence The Name of God wherever they are. But we Christians need to hallow The Name of Our God even more. Do not keep silent.

Isaiah 62:1-2 *"For Zion's sake will I not hold my peace, and for Jerusalem's sake I will not rest, until the righteousness thereof go forth as brightness, and the salvation thereof as a lamp that burneth. And the Gentiles shall see thy righteousness, and all kings thy glory: and thou shalt be called by a new name, which the mouth of the LORD shall name".*

When we pray "Hallowed be Thy Name," we are acknowledging God's supreme holiness, greatness, and majesty. It's a reminder that God's name embodies His perfect nature, love, power, and authority. We are asking for God to be honoured, not only in our own lives but also in the world, that His name would be treated with the utmost reverence and never be taken lightly.

Moreover, this part of the prayer calls for us to live in a way that reflects the holiness of God, meaning our lives should honour Him. We are aligning ourselves with His purposes, inviting His holiness to shape our actions, thoughts, and words, so that in everything we do, God's name is glorified and respected. It's both a declaration and a personal commitment to live in a way that upholds the sanctity of God's name.

We begin by honouring and reverencing God's name in our daily prayers, worshiping Him in Spirit and in truth, before presenting any requests or petitions.

Matthew 6:10 ***"Your Kingdom come. Your will be done on earth as it is in Heaven".***

This is the main reason why we gather massively in churches, crusades and in all other Christian meetings to display our convictions, to strategize on the establishment of the Kingdom of God on earth.

If you say you do not like going to church every Sunday, I will recommend you start learning to get used to the Church assembly every Sunday here on earth if at all you would like to go to Heaven for Eternity. In Heaven you will be in the Church for Eternity, not just sitting down and listening to the preacher, but worshipping and singing Halleluiah to The KING of kings for Eternity with joy.

We need to wholeheartedly embrace God's will with joy and willingness. We are called to submit to His Word, obey His commandments, and follow His statutes and precepts so that His will is fulfilled in us personally, then within the Church, and ultimately throughout the whole earth. Only then can we truly say that we are obedient children of God.

However, it is not by our own power or ability. This is why, in our prayers, we must continually seek God's grace and strength, recognizing that we are merely vessels in His hands. We should ask our Father to make us instruments through which His will is done and His Kingdom is manifested here on earth. It's essential to pray for the wisdom and capability to be useful in every area that contributes to the advancement of His Kingdom, whether through our actions, words, or the lives we touch. By seeking His divine empowerment, we position ourselves to fulfil His purpose. May the Lord guide and help us in all we do, in Jesus' Precious Name.

Matthew 6: 11 *"Give us this day our daily bread"*.

We often ask God for our daily bread and provision, but there are times when some forget to do so. In moments of urgent need, many instinctively turn to relatives, acquaintances, or connections who have the resources, reaching out to them first and depending on their help. Others may turn to banks or financial institutions for loans, which can lead to greater financial burdens. Some may even take on additional jobs, sacrificing precious time with their families.

However, it is important to remember that the Lord is our ultimate Provider, the Giver of all good things. If God chooses to use family or friends to meet our needs, He will stir their hearts to offer assistance. God may also work through banks to support your business or through your salary to bless you. But above all, we must first **ask God in prayer**. He knows our needs and will provide according to His will.

3 John 1: 2 *"Beloved, I wish above all things that thou mayest prosper and be in health, even as thy soul prospereth".* The Lord has promised to supply all your needs. Philippians 4: 19

"But my God shall supply all your need according to his riches in glory by Christ Jesus".

We all know people who work tirelessly—those who have taken out loans to start businesses, or have connections with wealthy individuals. Yet, true and lasting blessings come only when God's hand is upon you, for His blessings come without added sorrow.

I remember a sister in Amsterdam who worked incredibly hard, from 8 a.m. to 6 p.m. every day, all while raising three young children. She was also serving faithfully in the church, but her husband was unemployed. Despite earning a good salary, she was constantly in financial need. At one point, she took a loan to cover some expenses, but after a few months, while some needs were met, she found herself burdened by debt and still facing financial pressures. She came to us for counsel, and we said to her, "Sister, your three children need you, and you are exhausted.

Could you consider taking a moment to prayerfully reflect on your life and that of your family, and spend more time with God? He will surely guide you. By God's grace, the sister took this counsel to heart. She left her previous job and drew closer to God in prayer. I still remember the day she came to me and said, "Pastor, praise God, I prayed today." I responded, "Amen."

In just a few months, God opened a door for her to join a company that allowed her to work from home. Her schedule became more balanced, her children happier and healthier, and her husband found a job that fulfilled him, growing more loving in the process. With more focus on her new job, she began earning a better income, which, together with her husband's, covered the family's needs. Truly, God took control of the entire situation.

God is the source of all provision. He owns everything we need and will supply all your needs in Jesus' Name. Our God: Jehovah Jireh is the Great Provider. He leads us into abundance, for all hidden riches belong to Him, and He teaches us how to thrive.

Matthew 6: 12 *"And forgive us our trespasses as we forgive those who trespass against us"*.

1 John 1: 9 *"If we confess our sins, He is faithful and just to forgive us our sins, and to cleanse us from all unrighteousness"*.

Confessing our sins is an acknowledgment of our human frailty and imperfections. It is a humble recognition that we fall short, yet in our weaknesses, God's strength is perfected, as the scripture reminds us:

(2 Corinthians 12: 9) *"His strength is made perfect in our weakness"*. He is the merciful and gracious God, the only One who has the power to forgive sins. His love is boundless, and His grace extends to all who seek it.

In this, we are reminded that there is no need to create enmity with anyone, regardless of disagreements or past mistakes. When we err, the path forward is not in harbouring bitterness but in seeking reconciliation and making amends. It is always better to seek peace, to right wrongs, and to cultivate a heart of forgiveness.

What deeply concerns me is when people, knowingly or unknowingly, position themselves as adversaries of Christianity. In doing so, they may not realize they are resisting God Himself. It is essential to approach these matters with caution, recognizing that opposing the faith might mean opposing the very One who seeks to save and redeem. True strength is found not in resisting God, but in aligning with His will and accepting His love.

God told Abraham: Genesis 12: 3 *"And I will bless them that bless thee, and curse him that curseth thee: and in thee shall all families of the earth be blessed"*.

God is not pleased when His children are persecuted, threatened, or maltreated unjustly. But as believers, our role is not to retaliate or hold onto resentment. Instead, we are called to forgive wholeheartedly and keep walking with God, who is the ultimate judge and defender. He knows how to bring justice in

His perfect timing, and when we choose forgiveness, we disarm the enemy's ability to accuse us before God.

I find great joy in forgiving others quickly, because I have personally witnessed God's powerful hand of protection and vindication in my life. There have been moments when people opposed God's work in me, but after God visited them, I often felt a desire to reach out, to encourage them to turn to His love and align with His will. However, some hearts remain hardened. In those moments, God gently reminds me, "Leave them to Me. If they oppose what you do in My Name, they oppose Me, and I will handle them."

Through these experiences, I've learned to trust God's wisdom and timing, knowing that He is more than capable of defending His children. My focus remains on walking in love, letting God fight the battles.

There was a man who actively opposed God's work when we were establishing a new branch of our church in Amsterdam. After a few months, he fell into depression, left the church, and was admitted to a psychiatric hospital. We felt compassion for him and reached out, calling to minister to him over the phone. But in his psychotic state, he kept repeating, "he have chosen the path of evil, and that's where he intended to stay."

I prayed for him, asking, "Lord, please help him." God spoke to me, saying, "I will heal him in My time, but for now, stay away from him."

Then the Lord reminded me, "Do you remember the prodigal son? When he left his father's house with his inheritance, his father didn't go after him. He didn't search for him or send anyone to bring him back. It wasn't until the son realized the emptiness of his life away from his father that he returned on his own, at the right time."

The Lord continued, "Do you remember Nebuchadnezzar? When he refused to acknowledge Me as the One who elevates, he was humbled and became like a beast. No one from his palace went looking for him in the wilderness. He wasn't brought back until he had completed his time there and finally recognized Me. Only then was he restored as king of Babylon."

God concluded, "Leave this man alone. I will break him, and he will not learn until he returns from his wilderness experience. Then he will know that I am God, I protect and defend My servants and My work."

After a long and difficult year, a man was finally healed from a severe affliction. For the entire year, he was considered mentally unstable and treated with psychiatric protocols. Yet, it was only through God's intervention, in response to the prayers of the Church, that he was fully restored.

This highlights the importance and power of forgiveness. When we choose not to hold grudges or seek revenge against those who persecute us, but instead forgive and entrust them to God, we invite the Lord of hosts to fight on behalf of His children and His Church. Moreover, when we forgive, God, in turn, forgives our sins.

In the wilderness, Korah, Dathan, and Abiram stood against Moses and Aaron, challenging their leadership. They stirred up a rebellion, convincing 250 well-known and respected leaders from among the Israelites to join them. But their actions displeased God, leading to a tragic outcome for all involved. The story of their defiance is recorded in Numbers 16:1-3, 31-35. The account serves as a solemn reminder of the consequences of rebelling against God's appointed leaders.

It is crucial that we genuinely pray for our enemies and forgive them from our hearts. Holding onto grudges or seeking revenge will only weigh us down, and it may not end well for those who have wronged us. However, forgiving them does not mean aligning ourselves with their destructive ways or falling into the same traps they may have set for us. When they begin to face the consequences of their actions, we should not join them in their downfall.

Instead, forgiveness involves letting go of bitterness while wisely asking God to extend His mercy toward them. It requires discernment; praying for their redemption and transformation, rather than standing in judgment. We trust that God, in His infinite wisdom, will deal with them justly. Our role is to walk in love and compassion, lifting our enemies before God, and seeking their well-being without compromising our own integrity or boundaries.

In doing so, we free ourselves from the weight of resentment and allow God to work in both their lives and ours. True forgiveness is not passive; it is a deliberate act of grace that reflects the mercy we have received from God, wisely extending that same mercy to others, no matter how deeply they may have wronged us.

Proverbs 4:7 *"Wisdom is the principal thing; therefore get wisdom: and with all thy getting get understanding."*

Ecclesiastes 10:10. *"... wisdom is profitable to direct."*

Matthew 6:13a **"And do not lead us into temptation, But deliver us from the evil one."**

Evil is a deeply entrenched system orchestrated by satan, which first infiltrated humanity in the Garden of Eden. This corruption began when man, under the deceptive influence of satan: the embodiment of all evil, disobeyed God's command by eating the forbidden fruit. From that moment, humanity became entangled in a cycle of sin and separation from God. The objective of the enemy was to distort the divine order, leading mankind into rebellion against their Creator. What was initially a single act of disobedience set in motion the spread of evil, not just in the Garden but across generations, shaping human history with consequences that persist to this day; Thank God for the Redemptive Power of the Blood of Jesus Christ.

The event in Eden was not merely an act of defiance but the beginning of a greater spiritual conflict, where satan sought to undermine God's perfect creation by introducing sin into the world. Through this act, evil gained a foothold in human nature, making it a universal struggle for mankind to resist temptation and strive toward righteousness.

Evil, therefore, is not just a concept; it is a powerful force actively working to lead people away from God's truth and into spiritual darkness.

Genesis 2: 17a *"but from the tree of the knowledge of good and evil ..."* The forbidden fruit is the fruit of the knowledge of good and evil.

Before the sin of Adam and Eve, they only knew good and were unaware of evil. However, after eating the fruit from the tree, they gained the knowledge of evil and were faced with choices that only God should make. Similarly, when you engage in evil actions, you are following the example of Adam and Eve, obeying the evil one and demonstrating that, in that moment, you are serving the evil voice. For you become a servant to whomever you choose to obey.

Romans 6: 16 *"Know ye not, that to whom ye yield yourselves servants to obey, his servants ye are to whom ye obey; whether of sin unto death, or of obedience unto righteousness?"*

Many people today are aware that they are living outside of God's will. In response, they often resort to cunning, deceitful, and even devilish schemes to lead others astray.

Some time ago, there was an elderly man named Michael who worshipped with us at our church in France. He loved God, but he had a habit of drinking wine excessively—so much so that he rarely drank water. Wine was his daily drink. On most Sundays, he would come to the church service having already consumed wine.

One day, I approached him and said, "Sir, we usually avoid drinking alcohol before attending church. While I cannot forbid you from drinking, I kindly ask that you refrain from doing so when coming to church for your own sake and for the sake of others who may be spiritually weaker."

He responded, "I understand."

However, the following Sunday, he arrived at church drunk again. I hesitated to bring myself to repeat the same remark to him directly, so I took it to prayer. The Holy Spirit said, 'Keep confronting Michael until he stops.'

I thought to myself, 'I don't want to embarrass this man, I respect him but I must obey the Holy Spirit.' Then the Lord spoke again: 'If he isn't ashamed to drink before coming to church, why should you be reluctant to kindly tell him to stop? Be courageous. Stop him before he corrupts the entire church. At that point I recalled the scripture in James 4:7

"Submit yourselves therefore to God. Resist the devil, and he will flee from you".

The only language that satan comprehends is the language of resistance. It is through steadfast opposition and unwavering determination that we thwart his plans. When we resist his temptations and stand firm in our faith, we communicate our refusal to be swayed by his deceit. In this spiritual battle, it is our resilience and persistence that serve as a powerful declaration, sending a clear message that we will not yield to darkness.

Matthew 11:12 *"And from the days of John the Baptist until now the kingdom of heaven suffereth violence, and the violent take it by force"*

Sometime later, I found the opportunity to approach Michael once more. I said to him, "You are an elder in this assembly, and we hold you in high regard. We deeply value the contributions you have made to this church. However, we also ask that you show respect to us by setting a proper example. If you cannot abstain from alcohol before the Service, I kindly ask that you consider finding another congregation."

Upon hearing this, Michael became very angry. His frustration was evident, and he left the Church in a fit of emotion. Despite his departure, we did not give up on him. We continued to lift him up in prayer, trusting that God would work in his heart.

Six months passed, and to our surprise, Michael returned to the church. This time, he was a changed man; sober, clean, and filled with renewed zeal. He approached me, along with the entire church, expressing his heartfelt gratitude for the grace and patience extended to him. He said: "Yahweh spoke to me after I left, urging me to return, humble myself, and take responsibility for the young brothers who looked up to me. He instructed me to guide them in studying the Bible and to be a positive example."

From that moment on, Michael became one of the most dedicated and effective Bible teachers in our assembly. His transformation was a powerful testimony by the grace of God. That is what God requires from us: Persistence in prayer.

Another example involves a man who was reportedly preying on single women in various churches, luring them into sinful relationships. Outwardly, he appeared to have a perfect life: he had a wife and two children, and they lived as a loving family in Montpellier. However, one day, he abruptly abandoned his family, moving into a small studio apartment elsewhere in the city to carry out his deceptive mission in secret.

Despite leaving his home, he maintained the appearance of a devoted husband and father. He would still be with his family every day, each morning, he would take his children to school. However, he refused to live with them under the same roof, choosing instead to lead a double life, hiding his true intentions.

His scheme revolved around infiltrating churches every Sunday, pretending to be a devout Christian. He would act as though he were filled with the Holy Spirit, presenting himself as a "born-again" believer. His goal was to target vulnerable, single women in the congregation. With charm and deceit, he would build trust, often telling these women that he was divorced and searching for a new wife. Believing his lies, the women would enter into relationships with him, convinced of his sincerity.

He was patient and methodical, spending months building a relationship with each woman. However, once he is tired of one relationship, he would suddenly disappear, leaving the woman heartbroken and confused. His next move would be to find another church, where he would repeat the same pattern with another unsuspecting woman. The first woman would eventually discover that he had moved on to another church and another victim.

To him, this was all part of the plan, and he found amusement in the distress he caused. His conscience was seared, and he seemed to take pleasure in knowing that he could manipulate these women without consequence. Over the course of a few years, he had established a notorious reputation, having formed and abandoned numerous short-term relationships across different churches in the city.

Eventually, his behaviour became so widely known that pastors across Montpellier began to issue warnings to their congregations, advising the single women to be wary of him.

His photograph was displayed in numerous churches, almost like that of a wanted criminal. However, beneath his image, a warning was inscribed in French: *"Attention, coureur de jupons terrible dans les Eglises"*, which translates to "Beware, terrible womanizer in churches."

This public exposure of his immoral behaviour led to his downfall. Confronted by the truth, he eventually repented, surrendering his life back to God. He gave his heart to Christ and returned to his family, turning away from his sinful ways.

This example serves as a reminder of the spiritual battles we face, even within the walls of the church. The forces of darkness can infiltrate not just the world outside but also the sacred spaces of worship. Temptation is not confined to secular settings; it can also exist within the church itself.

My prayer is that, as our faithful God protects us from falling into temptation, we should remain vigilant. May we be discerning enough to recognize and expose the works and schemes of the enemy so that we do not succumb to temptation, in the powerful Name of Jesus Christ.

Matthew 6:13b *For Thine is the Kingdom and the Power and the Glory forever. Amen.*

The Kingdom, the Power and the Glory belong to Our Lord God. He is Our maker, and The Creator of heaven and earth. The whole world is in His Hand. God made all things to His Glory!

The Kingdom: *God's Sovereign Rule*

The declaration, "For Thine is the Kingdom," affirms that all authority belongs to God. In this context, "Kingdom" refers to God's sovereign rule over the universe. It is a reminder that everything, both visible and invisible, is under the reign of the Almighty. This phrase acknowledges God's ownership over all creation, and in prayer, we recognize His ultimate authority.

As believers, when we pray, we align ourselves with God's Kingdom purposes. Jesus Christ here speaks of the Kingdom of God, encouraging us to live in a way that reflects Kingdom values: righteousness, justice, and love. By ending the Lord's Prayer with this statement, we submit to God's will, acknowledging that His plans and purposes are higher than ours.

In the creative power of prayer, recognizing God's Kingdom empowers the believer to trust in His perfect plan. Praying with an awareness of God's Kingdom invites His rule into every area of our lives, giving us the strength to believe that His ways are best, no matter the circumstances. This Kingdom mindset transforms our prayers from self-focused requests to God-focused petitions, where we desire to see His reign manifest in our lives and in the world.

The Power: *The Source of All Ability*

The phrase "and the Power" means all power belongs to God. In prayer, we tap into this divine power, recognizing that God is the source of all strength and ability. Human strength is limited, but God's power is infinite. When we pray, we are not simply speaking words; we are connecting with the One who has the power to change situations, heal the sick, restore relationships, and bring the impossible to pass.

In prayer, this acknowledgment of God's power reminds us that we are not praying out of our own capabilities. We are vessels through which God's power flows. This creates a sense of dependence on God, freeing us from the pressure of trying to make things happen in our strength. Instead, we can trust that God's power will be demonstrated in our lives.

This truth amplifies the creative power of prayer. When we recognize that God's power is available to us, it emboldens our prayers. We are no longer limited by what we can see or what we think is possible; we begin to pray with the understanding that "with God, all things are possible" (Matthew 19:26). Prayer becomes a dynamic force for bringing God's will to pass because His power is at work behind our words.

In Psalms 8: 3-9, David said: *"When I consider Thy heavens, the work of Thy Fingers, the moon and the stars, which Thou hast ordained; what is man, that Thou art mindful of him ? and the son of man, that Thou visitest him ? For Thou hast made him a little lower than the angels, and hast crowned him with glory and honour. Thou madest him to have dominion over the works of Thy hands; Thou hast put all things under his feet: All sheep and oxen, yea, and the beasts of the field; The fowl of the air, and the fish of the sea, and whatsoever passeth through the paths of the seas. O LORD our Lord, how excellent is Thy Name in all the earth!".* *Amen*

The Glory: *The Ultimate Purpose*

"And the Glory" points us to the ultimate purpose of all things: to glorify God. Everything in the universe exists to display God's glory, His infinite beauty, and majesty. When we pray, we recognize that God alone deserves all the glory for the answers we receive. Whether He provides a miraculous solution or gives us the grace to endure, it is all for His glory.

In this part of the prayer, we shift our focus from ourselves to God, understanding that the glory of God is the end goal of our lives and prayers. When we pray creatively, seeking God's glory, we pray beyond our personal desires. Our prayers become opportunities for God to showcase His character, love, and power to the world.

This perspective reshapes how we approach prayer. Instead of seeking our own recognition, we desire that God be magnified. We trust that whatever answer He provides will bring glory to His name. This is the essence of the creative power of prayer: it leads to transformation, not just of circumstances but of hearts, as we learn to give God the glory in all things.

Forever: *The Eternal Nature of God's Kingdom, Power, and Glory*

The phrase *"forever"* seals this verse by pointing to the Eternal nature of God's Kingdom, power, and glory. God's reign, strength, and majesty are not fleeting; they are everlasting. This gives us confidence in prayer because we know that we are standing on a foundation that will never fail. His Kingdom will endure, His power will never diminish, and His glory will shine for all eternity.

In this eternal view, prayer becomes an act of faith, trusting that God's eternal purposes are being worked out in our lives. We may not always see immediate results, but we can rest in the assurance that God's Kingdom and power are at work beyond time, bringing His eternal will to pass. This eternal perspective frees us to pray with boldness, knowing that God's answers to our prayers are part of His grand, unending plan.

Amen: *The Affirmation of Faith*

The final word, *"Amen,"* is more than a closing statement. It is an affirmation of faith, meaning "so be it." By saying "Amen," we declare our trust in God's Kingdom, power, and glory. We affirm that we believe what we have prayed and trust that God will answer according to His will.

In the context of the creative power of prayer, *"Amen"* is a statement of agreement with God's purposes. It signifies that we are standing in faith, trusting that God will do what He has promised. As we close our prayers with *"Amen,"* we leave our requests in God's hands, believing that He will bring His will to pass in our lives and in the world.

This profound ending to the Lord's Prayer reminds us of the greatness of the God we serve and the power of prayer. When we acknowledge God's Kingdom, power, and glory in our prayers, we are tapping into divine realities that transform our lives and the world around us.

INVITATION

INVITATION

Our righteousness is of the Lord. It is therefore necessary for us to be part of the body of Christ and to have a personal relationship with the Lord to become the children of God.

John 1: 12-13 *"But as many as received Him, to them gave He power to become the sons of God, even to them that believe on His name: Which were born, not of blood, nor of the will of the flesh, nor of the will of man, but of God."*

Do you want to be confident in your spiritual battles in prayer, do you want to give your heart and your life to God so He can dwell in you for ever? You can pray the following prayer to the Lord.

Heavenly Father, I come to You through Your only begotten Son Jesus Christ. I am very sorry for my sins, I repent of my sins and iniquities. Please forgive me, cleanse me from all my unrighteousness through the Blood of Your Son Jesus Christ. I want You to come into my heart and save me. Lord Jesus, I believe you died on the cross for my sins and was raised again for my justification. I receive You as the Lord and Master of my life. I ask You to lead and guide me every day in Your Word and I ask for the power to obey you. I choose to obey you and follow Your will for my life. Thank You Lord for coming into my heart. Thank You Holy Spirit for writing my name in the Lamb's book of Life. In Jesus' Name I pray. Amen.

If you are a Christian already and you want to enter into the victorious life of Christ, to be set free from the powers of darkness and from the dominion of sin. You want to renew you commitment and covenant with the Lord you can likewise pray the above prayer.

If you need to agree in prayer with a minister to help you more in your prayer life and in your spiritual battles, write to the addresses below or call us, and we shall be delighted to assist you more in the Name of Our Lord Jesus Christ.

CONTACT

All our contact details can be found in the website: www.shekinahevangelicalchurch.com

ABOUT THE AUTHOR

The Author of this book; Pastor Mariana Vanstipelen got born again while finishing her Master's Degree in the Faculty of Arts (Linguistics) and Religion, Windhoek University.

She gave herself totally as a disciple of the Lord Jesus-Christ and a student of the Word of God Which she preferred above all subjects.

She speaks eight languages and is committed to using them to reach the nations with the Word of God.

Married and mother of two: Eunice and Joshua, Pastor of the Shekinah Evangelical Church, Mariana presently resides in The Netherlands as speaker and author of numerous books and collections.

TO GOD BE THE GLORY.

OTHER BOOKS BY
THE SAME AUTHOR

1. Biblical Principles of Long Life
2. Converting Mistakes to Miracles
3. Seven Ways God Answers Prayers
4. 70 Kinds of Prayers
5. Prayer for Healing
6. The Impact of Fasting in Prayer
7. Faith Versus Fear
8. Forgive
9. A Happy Christian
10. Jesus-Christ, the Bread of Life
11. Jesus-Christ, the Word of God
12. Power to Prosper
13. The Fruit of the Spirit
14. The Hem of His Garment
15. The Holy Spirit
16. The King of kings
17. The Mantle of Power
18. The Rhema of God
19. The Shekinah of God

BLESSINGS

*As you complete this journey through The Creative Power of Prayer,
I encourage you to embrace the life of powerful, transformative prayer
that God has called you to. May the insights, teachings, and reflections
in these pages deepen your relationship with God, strengthen your spirit,
and ignite a passion for prayer that touches every area of your life.*

*If this book has blessed you, we would love to hear from you.
Your testimony could encourage others and be a powerful reminder
of God's work through prayer. Feel free to share with us how these
principles have impacted your life.*

*And if you are seeking support through prayer, remember that you don't
walk this path alone. We welcome your prayer requests, standing with you
in faith as we believe in God's promises. As Jesus said in Matthew 18:19
"If two of you on earth agree about anything they ask for, it will be done
for them by my Father in heaven." Together, let us believe for miracles,
breakthroughs, and the fulfilment of God's plans.*

*May you continue to grow in grace, knowing that you are blessed,
highly favoured, and deeply loved by our Heavenly Father.*

NOTES

www.ingramcontent.com/pod-product-compliance
Lightning Source LLC
Chambersburg PA
CBHW070830120626
46556CB00002B/704